Love

& OBEY

THE WORLD'S BEST FEMALE LED
RELATIONSHIP GUIDE FOR THE WORLD'S BEST
WOMEN BECAUSE WE ARE WORTH IT!

Marisa Rudder

All of Marisa Rudder's Bestselling Books are available on Amazon:

Love & Obey, Real Men Worship Women, Oral Sex For Women, Cuckolding, Spanking, Chastity, and Turning Point.

Please contact Marisa Rudder with any questions: Email: femaleledrelationshipbook@gmail.com

Printed in the United States of America Publisher's Cataloging-in-Publication data

ISBN #978-0-9991804-6-4

You can find out more about the Love & Obey Female Led Lifestyle and all my books on my website: www.loveandobey.com

Or follow me on social media:

FACEBOOK

https://www.facebook.com/femaleledrelationships

TWITTER

https://twitter.com/loveandobeybook

INSTAGRAM

https://www.instagram.com/femaleledrelationships

YOUTUBE

https://www.youtube.com/channel/UCkX3wmd934WR103hStbzb
iQ?view_as=subscriber

Dedication

I would like to dedicate this book to all the strong, brave ladies, who have the courage to explore Female Led Relationships, especially as it goes against everything that the society teaches us. It is my hope that this book will motivate you to dream big dreams in life, and it is my hope that you will find romance with a gentleman, who will love, obey and serve you, and make you feel like a Queen Mother. It is my desire that every male will experience the joy of being a gentleman and the nobility of chivalry by entering into a loving Female Led Relationship, and experiencing the state of sexual and emotional ecstasy, created by Female authority, at some point in his life.

Introduction

A lot has changed in the world, ranging from the littlest things to the biggest of things. Relationships have changed over time. Men no longer treat the womenfolk the same. The respect for our partners has dwindled. This begs for the question; "Is chivalry dead?" Are there any more gentlemen left in the world?

I was riding the subway a few days ago, and something struck me, while I was standing on the platform, waiting for the doors to open. Men were primed to rush ahead of women and old people. Once inside, they rushed in, grabbed all the seats, leaving a number of women and older ladies to hang on tightly to the poles, which prevented them from falling over. The cliche, 'ladies first' didn't seem to hold any more meaning to them. I wondered when the society came to a twist. When did men stop standing aside, to allow women to go through a walkway first, or take a seat in the bus while they stand?

Men no longer deem it fit to open doors for ladies, pull out chairs, open car-doors, or even offer to help carry their heavy luggage. Much less any grand gestures, like lay down their coats so a woman doesn't get dirty. These were normal occurrences in the 30's, 40's, and 50's, but you will barely see it happen today.

Despite this being the norm, I still don't believe chivalry is dead. Instead, I think it has just been cast aside and as such, needs to be rekindled. I feel that it is very important that women take the lead, just as they are doing in many other areas of life, and bring back chivalry. Insist on it. But create a modern version.

Let's take a moment and look at what chivalry is.

Chivalry comes from the medieval knightly system with a specific religious, moral, and social code. It was the code under which, knights, noblemen, and horsemen, collectively lived. Governed by this code of chivalry, an ideal man was expected to be courageous, honorable, courteous, just, and always ready to help the weak. A chivalrous man was always required to display courteous behavior, especially towards women.

So, if chivalry is dead, who should we blame?

We can only blame ourselves, that we are no longer treated with the respect and the courtesy that we deserve, by men. In the struggle for our independence as women, we have come to forfeit vital things, like chivalry. Today, a woman accepts that men will not hold doors, will rush into a train and take all the seats, are served dinner first, or get a better pay for the same job.

We accept that our role is still to get all the housework done, take care of the kids, work in our day job, and handle 90 percent of couples' duties. We allow the new norms to get solidified - split the cheque on a first date, have sex early in a relationship, allow men to be sexually satisfied, while we sometimes and most often, are not even close to having an orgasm. Some of us have allowed abuse to happen in our relationships - mental and physical. We women, allow this to become perfectly normal, and left un-contradicted. Well, I had a radical thought, not too long ago. Why does it have to be this way? Why can't women have it all? We can have chivalry, respect, and commitment and yet, be completely in charge. This is what I'm going to explore in this book. There should be a revolution which directs men to return to being chivalrous, by placing the woman's needs first. I will push the envelope even more to say, women run households, handle the kids, care for aging parents, have demanding careers, head corporations and rule countries. So, all of this suggest perhaps, we are the ones to determine the rules of the relationship, and take charge in a new union called the Female-Led Relationship. In this relationship, men will love, serve and obey us first, place our needs first, and submit to our lead. We, in turn, must take our rightful place to teach our husbands, boyfriends and lovers, about these new rules so that we everywhere, are more satisfied in our relationships, sex life, at work and at home, and no longer put the needs of men first. Because the truth is that, we cannot make our men happy if we are not happy. If we are honest, most of us will agree that we are left unsatisfied in our relationships. And why? Because there is a growing movement of female power in the world, in the workplace and in the society, but not a whole lot has changed in our private lives, in the bedroom, or at home. So, I think it's time to change. I've always loved the movie, "Inception". It depicts the idea that if we get deep inside the layers of the mind, we can change our whole thinking, outlook and personality, by planting the new thought, deep deep inside. Then, like a weed, it will spread and grow, and replace the old thinking. This is what needs to happen with the Female Led

Relationship. By starting at home and in our relationships with men, we begin to create an entirely new paradigm, where women take their rightful place, in the drivers seat. Let's face it; Mother Nature is a driving force, so even at the heart of powerful forces in the universe, there is the female power at work.

The term "Happy Wife, Happy Life" is not just true; it's essential. Women are the head of the household, and are really the head of the family. It is interesting that hundreds of years ago, this was always true, but somehow, running a household and caring for the family became a position of subservience, when all along, it was the key to a proper functioning society. A dysfunctional family is as a result of the lack of a female, taking charge and having the ability to run the household. Its not an easy job. But if a woman is unable to fulfill her role as the head of the family, it suffers. The household is the family unit, and it's mandatory for a well-run society to have good household and family units. It goes to the core of the society. We learn our first habits from our family. We also learn how to relate to each other, from what we learn in our family. Women have always had the job of keeping the family together and oftentimes, the mother child bond is the most important in every child's life. Since this is such a crucial key necessity for the functioning of the family which extends to society, a woman needs to feel happy and satisfied, even placed on a pedestal by her man and having her needs met, daily. Then, she is free to be able to take on, the responsibilities of running the household, holding down a demanding career, caring for aging parents, and all the other duties that is demanded of her. This is where a female-led relationship has so many advantages. It's been my experience that female-led marriages last longer, and the family unit sticks together. Just because women now partake in all areas of the industry and the workplace, doesn't mean she is any less powerful in the home. The female force is needed in both areas. Think of a workplace which has only men. Sports like Football and Hockey. What do we witness? - Brawn, men butting heads, fights, aggressive behavior. Even in history, it took Queen Elizabeth to herald in a new era of beauty, and the arts in the Renaissance. I'm always amazed when I see the era when men were the only ones who ruled. It was harsh, and cold, and lacked any beauty. That's not to say that all men are unable to create beauty, but I believe that it's the men who tap into their female side that are capable of doing this.

This lends credibility to the fact that the female power is real, and it is a power that we, as women, need to cultivate at home and at work. The ancient idea that women needed to be more male, is archaic. When women first entered the corporate world, they had to dress in corporate structured suits, just like men. This practice still continues. Why ? We don't need to look and act more male to be powerful. We can be leaders, and still exert or own female power. That is my hope from this book; to show that women can take their rightful position as head of the household, and be a leader in the relationship as well, while maintaining their natural feminine power.

We can also look at the basic laws of the world that can sometimes, favor women. Without a woman's consent for a sexual act, it would be considered rape- a crime. So too, a woman, even in the simplest of gestures, should give her consent before her man can act. What I hope to do in this book, is establish a set of rules and framework to help women and men, who want to be in a female-led relationship, thrive and create something very special. I have consulted many different resources, as well as my own personal experience, to develop much of the instruction and advice I will offer. I know that this type of relationship and living that I suggest may spark a lot of controversy, but, I believe that in the end, women who are happy, satisfied and productive, will be greater assets to the society, than if we felt neglected, powerless, victimized and weak. We must take up the torch, just as we do on women's marches. I believe there has never been a better time, nor will there be a better time to create a great change for women. So too, in our relationships, we must demand what we want, instruct, and lead our men. Let's face it; men were never good at reading a woman's mind, and many have been spoiled and coddled by their mothers, so they pretty much do what they want and everyone must accept it. Ever noticed when you are trying to discuss a problem with a man, he feels its okay to roll his eyes, or tune you out? I often wondered when this behavior became acceptable, but, I later learned that it's the difference in communication styles. When men are hanging out at a bar, they bond with their friends, even if they are going through challenges. Unlike women, they do not sit around and discuss personal issues that they are having. Why? Because of the difference in communication styles. It's a well-known fact that men don't communicate as well as women do. So, even in our most basic need, which is to communicate, men are not trained. We want to talk out the problem and receive an open ear; they are not able to do this. So, we are left unfulfilled, unheard, feeling ignored and angry. Even though this is our primary method of releasing stress and dealing with challenges. Women need to talk, and men can't communicate. This is the fundamental problem in relationships, but there is hope. The female-led relationship is different. It puts the responsibility of training men, helping them to understand how to relate to women, as well as the decision-making in the family, firmly on the shoulders of women. So, if we want to be in the driver's seat, we must help our men daily, to satisfy our wishes, while we also provide direction. We do this by carefully choosing our words, and the exchange we have on a daily basis. I remind myself daily, that when we speak, we have the opportunity to be Martin Luther King or Hitler. Both were eloquent, and inspired millions of people. But one was driven by love, while the other was driven by fear. So, when we speak to our men, we want to inspire them with motivating speech and not derogatory comments. If we want the return of a gentleman, we need to coach him carefully.

The word, "gentle" refers to being kind, tender, sympathetic, considerate, understanding, compassionate, benevolent, good-natured, courteous and chivalrous. Let's face it; this is what we all want, whether we accept it or pretend to not care. We want a man to come home, and be understanding of our needs, attentive, listen to us, be helpful, open doors for us, carry heavy items for us, give us a back-rub, prepare us a bath, buy us little surprises, and satisfy our sexual needs first. Men can still work, control the finances, do the handy work, or protect us if needed. However, what has changed is that, he comes to understand that you are the queen and so, he must satisfy your desires, regardless of the circumstances around. It becomes one of his duties, and supersedes his duties at work. Lets face it, we are all very good at attending to everything that needs to get done for work. We get an email from our boss, and we drop everything to attend to it. So, because work is now creeping into the little family and personal time that we have, the relationship and personal life suffers. There needs to be a change. We all have to work, some probably longer than ever before; so, we need to create boundaries where work does not conflict with relationship or family time. This takes scheduling, monitoring, executing and real leadership from the head of the family - the woman. But, there needs to be co-operation from her man, to help the entire family build these healthy practices. In today's world where our phones often take precedence no matter where we are, work, home, out a restaurant, at the movies or exercising, it is extremely difficult to stick to those boundaries. How many times are we sitting on the couch with our man, and he is on his phone and you are on your phone? The little time you have to spend together has disappeared, and it's replaced with wasting of time, reading emails, texts, or on social media. The focus is now removed from your mate, to other distractions. This is where I believe that the breakdown of every relationship begins. This also tends to occur when we have been in the relationship or marriage for years, but they are habits which creep into the relationship which were not there during the "courting" phase. How many of us would allow the man we are with, on a first-date, to be on his phone during dinner. The first sight of him checking his phone, would send us into a tailspin, and there probably would not be a second date. Yet, we women, have allowed this to happen in our relationships. Many may say, this is not our faults, but as the head of the household, it is our responsibility to lay down the rules, which work to bring the family or the relationship together.

Ladies, you know deep down inside, that the Female Led Relationship is what you really want. You want a man who can satisfy all of your needs of friendship, support, communication, partnership and sexual needs. There is an old saying, "Men desire,

Women want to be desired." This is what we are missing. So, Chivalry and allowing men to do what they do best, while we gently lead them to love and obey us, will lead to a happier and much stronger, long-term marriages and relationship. Ladies, once you read my book, you will develop a clear picture of how to achieve a Female -Led Relationship in no time at all. This will lead to a lifetime of fulfillment and happiness for you and your man, and you will both enjoy the best sex you've ever had. Some couples prefer a very mild form of a Female -Led Relationship with just a couple of rules, while others desire a more intense form, following the full program of re-conditioning and re-programming for both. The important point is: there must be commitment from both you and your man, to fulfill your roles completely. Resistance should not be met with anger or resentment, as it will be a learning experience for both.

Table of Contents

CHAPTER ONE

--·—❦—·--

The Beginning

*I always believed that one woman's success could only help
another woman's success*

-Gloria Vanderbilt

My initial contact with the world of Female Led
Relationships was in early 2002. I was still in college,
and I was doing some research for a paper I was
working on; Human Sexuality.

On hearing about my research, a couple of my friends invited
me to attend some parties and group meetings that centered on
Female dominance, and male submission. The first group
meeting I attended had me feeling like a nervous wreck. As I
walked through the door and looked around, I discovered that it
was a predominantly male group. I was surprised, because I had
expected a room filled with women talking about feminism. The
room had about twenty people present, fifteen of them were

men. There was an introductory meeting for first timers, so nothing out of the ordinary or particularly strange happened that night; it was the people in this group that were explaining who they were, what their meetings stood for, and what it involved. My curiosity was piqued, and I found this subject of Female Dominance and Male Submission to be most fascinating. By the end of the night, I knew I would return. There was a social interaction after the meeting, and I mingled with some of the people, asking many questions. What I discovered was that many of these first- timers were men who wanted to be submissive in their relationships with women. They were in search of females, who would dominate them sexually, lead their relationships, and take control.

Since it was a sexually oriented group, there were some self-proclaimed dominant men present, but a majority of the males present at this meeting, wanted to be in the submissive role. I found this to be quite fascinating. I, a so-called feminist, had listened to several lectures about how women were struggling to gain equality in our society, but there was a room full of men, who willingly wanted to have women as their superiors. That meeting was a major turning point for me.

I was raised in the Caribbean islands of Trinidad and Tobago, a tropical paradise located about 100 miles off the coast of Venezuela. I attended all girls' Catholic school, and it is here I received all the standard patriarchal societal and religious programming that had indoctrinated me since I was a little girl. I have always been a spiritual person, a Christian, who believes in God and Jesus. I am thankful for my religious upbringing, however, the Catholic Church, and its male dominated hierarchy, force-fed me with a theology that made me view my gender as subservient. However, all around me were shining examples of women, who were in power. My mother was a strong female, leading her household, later to become a single parent, and my school was run by nuns who made all decisions. Myself and my peers, all females, were all top island scholars, strong-minded, smart, and full of ambition. This prejudice pervasive in Catholicism where the priest, a man, runs the church became a major stumbling block for me, as I tried to succeed in a so-called 'man's world.' On one hand, my all-girl's school was preaching female superiority, equality and feminism, but on the other hand, a contradiction to the customs in the Catholic teaching, where women were subservient and almost non-existent, as male Priests were the heads of the church and women were forced into the role of the nuns, who were barely seen during services. Feminism had always appealed to me. I was a top student and athlete, who felt she could do anything a man could do, just as well. I had many male friends during my formative years, and we played sports, and interacted as equals. So, I was unable to accept that women were subservient to men. I think a lot of ways, the thought never entered my consciousness. I simply refused to accept it. I discovered that women possessed a higher moral character, and a more superior intellect. My mother single-handedly ruled our family, picked up, and had to survive after my father left. Even though our Catholic God was a man and the priests were all men, it was really the Nuns who ran my Catholic School. So, everywhere in my life, women were influential teachers and leaders, who raised me from my earliest childhood memories. The highest shining example of female energy power is mother earth. Every living organism, and the entire world, is governed by a female energy which I consider to be the most powerful force over all others.

So, while I witnessed patriarchal dominance in society and in religion, my daily life showed me practical examples of capable Female leadership. New thoughts, philosophies, and ideologies about relationships, and the Female gender superiority, were starting to occupy my mind. Of course, I kept these ideas to myself. First, I was still that little Catholic girl at heart, and so, I wasn't yet comfortable with voicing these ideas. Secondly, we still live in a male dominated society, and I still needed to fit in. I was never an extrovert; I hadn't ever considered myself to be dominant. I certainly had never heard of Female Led Relationships or Loving Female Authority, but these Female Led parties, which I had been attending, were opening doors to a new and different world from what I knew. They had become a safe-haven for me to explore what I later realized was a force dormant inside of me. Once I found support from other men and women who shared the same views, I became much more comfortable. Here, we were free from the societal and religious expectations, norms and practices. Men were free to exhibit their submissive natures, and females were allowed to explore the part of them that had been locked-up for ages: dominance. We wouldn't face judgment or be frowned at, for giving in to what I was quickly becoming to recognize as a natural way of life.

During my late teenage years, my family moved to North America. By the time I was 16 years old, I was at the top of my school in academics, and working two part-time jobs. I eventually was accepted into the university to study engineering. This was yet, another experience in a male-dominated field, where I witnessed the number of women move from 10% of the class, to 30% in my year. Women were brilliant, right alongside men, learning and contributing. Engineering was a perfect breeding ground for me to develop many of my thoughts about female-led relationships, because I watched as many women took charge in group projects and assignments, even though they were the minority. They were not afraid to speak up and debate with professors, and many of the class conversations, in Engineering, were happening with female students.

Men were equally brilliant, but happy to allow us, the females, to lead in many of our assignments. My education in Engineering lasted 3 years and then, I switched to Information Technology and Commerce, still quite male dominated. So, all of this university experience set the ground-work for my new paradigm of female- led relationships. I would later leave all of my post-secondary education behind, and move into another male dominated field of fitness. Bodybuilding was the rage at this time, and as a female, to be accepted as strong and competent enough to train men, alongside the male trainer, I felt I had to look and be the part. So, I trained every day, for hours in a gym, developing a very muscular physique but I became one of the top personal trainers, earning a six figure income, right out of school, and being a sought after fitness guru. Training people to be better, healthier and more confident about life, has always been a passion of mine. Being a personal trainer was my perfect job- one that indulged my secret desire to train men to view women as superior, and to remind women of their ability to take charge in life and their relationships.

It gave me my first real taste of creating a framework for the female -led existence, as I gained intimate knowledge into men and women, and all of their experiences and challenges in the world. It was during many of my training sessions that many clients admitted many of their deepest feeling to me. While I would never betray the trainer client relationship, I soon gathered that both men and women had secrets of feeling unfulfilled in their relationships, which they buried, for the sake of keeping the family unit intact. I could see that many were struggling for years, with an emptiness which can occur when you are unable to reveal the unhappiness in the day to day interactions, and I believe that this is what led to the breakdown of marriages and divorces.

What I witnessed, having trained hundreds of clients, was that the clients in female-led relationships were much happier and often, were together longer. During my university years, I was invited back to several of the female -led parties and group meetings. While I managed to convince myself that I kept going to them purely for educational and research purposes, the fact was that I had become curious and interested in this alternative female-led lifestyle. Each week, I met more of the regulars, and while there were an increasing number of women attending, it was apparent that the submissive men were the driving force behind this group.

The men far outnumbered the women, so I became popular pretty quickly. As I socialized and conversed with the members of the Female -Led Relationship groups, enjoying their parties and get-togethers, I met many women in positions of power; one in particular, who invited me to a luncheon that's made up of exclusively successful business women. I accepted her invitation, and attended the dinner. There, I met women who were leaders in companies, their own businesses, and even in politics. Several had professions in male dominated fields, and many had male employees, who worked for them. The woman, who invited me to this luncheon, was a CEO of a very large corporation, and I formed a very close friendship with her, and learned much about being a female leader. The education I received about female leadership in the corporate world was invaluable.

As my research into the world of female leadership in the business world continued, I began to identify gradually, with this way of life. Similar to what happens with inception, a seed had been planted many years ago, and all of my experiences were now watering it and making it grow. The female led lifestyle seemed right and it worked. It wasn't easy to let go of my Catholic schooling in childhood, but it was all fading, and a new side of myself was emerging. I eventually realized that female equality was not the end game and that ultimately, women needed to rule relationships, businesses, governments, social groups and even nations. I began to call myself and my group of female friends, "Queens".

By my definition, a Queen believes that women are the superior sex over men. She thinks that society would be better served if it were governed by women, instead of men. A Queen is a female in a position of authority, in business and government. Societies, like the UK, have accepted the leadership of a queen; so why not all societies? A Queen believes that women and men are not equal, but rather, different. She believes that women possess more traits suited for leadership than men, and that she contains the qualities that are best fitted to be in a position of authority. The female, as the hero, is more popular now than ever; in movies quite recently, in huge blockbusters like Wonder Woman, Hunger Games, Divergent, James Bond and Atomic Blonde. This is significant because it means that it's becoming very accepted by both men and women. A Female Led Relationship can also become widely accepted.

After my education in Engineering, IT and Commerce, though I had no desire to work in my field, it prepared me to continue to develop and participate in the Female Led Relationship group. This became so important to me that I combined my love for fitness and relationships, and incorporated both into my practice. I suppose in essence, I was training both males and females, and I gained a deep insight into the psychology of both, and how they related to each other. In fitness, I attracted men, who enjoyed a woman in charge, and I also attracted women, who wanted to become more dominant and in control, by building up their bodies and their self-confidence. I was able to build a rather large client list, and this was the key to further my learning and understanding of this lifestyle. My experience creating programs, which helped people get results in fitness, could now be applied to creating programs for couples, in order to create a successful relationship. I still believe, from my experience with hundreds of clients, that Female Led Relationships work long-term.

So, what is unique about the Female Led Relationship? Why is it different? First, male domination has been accepted for centuries, so the idea of female led household has only recently become of interest. It has been studied in-depth in Marketing, where it is understood, that the head of the household is the woman, who makes many of the buying decisions. So, professionals in advertising and marketing, understand how crucial it is to target the female as the head of the household.

There is also a growing movement of women in the workforce, and more females in executive positions, in business and government. So, the idea of female leaders is certainly becoming more accepted, and it's only a matter of time before they are leaders in the relationship as well. This evolution has taken decades. Hilary Clinton's race for President was a giant step for women in power for North America and even back in the 80s, Margaret Thatcher's rise in the UK signified a grand step forward for women in power. There are now, many Prime Ministers and Presidents of large countries, who are women, and this is accepted. I see a similar emergence of the female-led relationship as the next evolutionary step for relationships. The Female Led Relationship really began as sexual and social desires of men submit themselves to the Females. But the Female Led Relationship has evolved now to much more, than sexual fantasy. It will become the next major movement.

A little over twenty years ago, I was introduced to the concept of Female Led Relationships at the meetings and parties. What was surprising were the number of men who wanted to be submissive. In fact, the overall numbers of men outnumbered the women in attendance, by ten to one. Since I was present at these parties and meetings to educate myself further in my studies of the Female Led Relationship, I interviewed some of the dominant women and submissive men in an informal manner. Being a rather curious and aggressive female, I found myself attracted to this unusual world. My curiosity in Female Led Relationships has developed into about two decades of studying and practicing this alternative lifestyle. I have educated myself about the subjects of Female Led Relationships and male submissive desires.

Based on my years of research, observation, and participation, I learned that there are sexual and social reasons why men have submissive desires toward women. I discovered that a person's core nature expresses itself sexually, through different sexual desires. To some people, a man that wishes to be on the bottom during intercourse is perverted. However, I have come to understand that this desire to have the woman on top stems from the same core desire. That desire is to be sexually dominated by a woman. It is expressed differently, but it is the same deep-rooted motivation. Not only that, but this nature can evolve, and the man that desires to be on the bottom during intercourse today, may very well develop a desire later on, to be in a Female Led Relationship.

From studying several Female Led Relationships, I learned about the core natures of both men and women. As a woman, who was raised in a traditionally male dominant Catholic society, it was a revelation to me to discover the natural desire for the dominance and supremacy of the Female over the male. This revelation became the key to unlocking and understanding all submissive desires of men. It matters not, how these desires are expressed through different fantasies. The root and the core of these are all the same; namely, the desire of the male gender is to be dominated and ruled by the Female sex. Therefore, no expression of this submissive nature surprises me or shocks me. I have heard it all from the males I have interviewed and counseled, and I have seen it all through my participation in the Female Led Relationship's lifestyle.

Some men want to worship the female by tending to her physical and sexual needs (body worship), while others want to be made into domesticated gentlemen. But the common thread with all these sexual and submissive desires is the longing for loving female authority, and this is the real definition of the Female Led Relationships. The woman as the loving female authority who leads, and the man wants to fulfill her desires. I believe it all stems from the original dominant woman, in every man's life; his mother. A man's mother has always held the highest spot in his heart; she is his supreme queen, and I believe that all men secretly desire to have a supreme queen in their life. That's why it is perfectly normal for mothers and daughters-in-law to be rivals. It's that desire to be in the most revered spot in a man's life. But, just as a mother has her place, the wife, mother and life-mate has an even more important role and we, as the primary woman in our man's life, must step into the role and take charge. We have often heard that a man will choose the woman who is most like his Mother to be his long-term mate and often, this is the case with men who want to be submissive. It is the longing for a female authority figure, who he can fulfill, is his long term goal. Men are providers. They know their role, and most men know that their role in the family is to provide and satisfy. They are raised with this reality, and it is ingrained. In the past, men would feel ashamed if he was unable to make more money, or have a better career than his woman. But times are changing, where it is acceptable for both men and women to make equal, and for women to sometimes, make more. But, the desire for men to serve the new most important woman in his life does not diminish, even if the society has deemed it okay for roles to change. Many couples who are new to the Female Led Relationship world, and experience where the man makes less than the woman or stays home with the kids, are unaware that to maintain the rules are still important. Often, there could be feelings of stress by a woman, knowing that she has to take charge in her career and home. But, in fact, just as a woman tending to household duties was still a lot of work, the same is true for men, who are taking care of kids at home. Why is this happening more often? Because it is a natural evolution of the relationship.

CHAPTER TWO

--—⬯⬯⬯—--

The Male State of Mind

There is an innate desire in many men to be dominated by a woman. I believe that they are born with this desire, and I also believe that this desire is enhanced through his childhood

experiences with his Female authority figures. He is carried in the womb of a woman, birthed into this world by a woman, nurtured at the breasts of a woman, pleasured by the loving hands of woman, and loved and comforted by a woman. There is a special bond between a young boy and his mother. Freud suggested that part of this is sexual in his famous "Oedipus Complex." Most of the time, a young boy is bathed, caressed, nurtured, and spanked by an adult. With divorce at 50%, many households are ruled by single women, who shapes his first experience with female authority. I believe this experience does not fade; it only strengthens as men mature. When boys reach adolescence, many begin to experiment with their sexuality, as they are curious and drawn to the Female, her beauty and her mysterious ways. Sometimes, when we examine young relationships between teenage boys and girls, we can see, in some cases, a real desire for the female to lead. Men can develop issues with intimacy if there are problems with these first relationship experiences with women. Females tend to develop faster than men; so even in teenage years, the more mature girls tend to exert some authority over men, and this forms a foundation for the relationship later on. Where it varies, is in the woman's role during sex.

In general, if men indulge in submission, especially during sex, they can become accustomed to being dominated by the female. The submission to female authority also extends to teacher-student relationships and then, into the workplace, where men are now managed and directed by more females in leadership positions. We see this depicted in TV shows like Suits, The Good Wife, CSI, The Brave with strong; aggressive females in power positions. Women now hold many upper management positions, with men being their subordinates. A real movement in the society is happening when media increases the portrayal of female leaders, and many movies depict stories of Female Led Relationships. So, more and more, males are being conditioned to accept this authority, and crave it in their relationships. Walk down many upscale and yuppie neighborhoods, and you will see the fathers, who opt to stay home and raise children, while their wives have demanding careers. There are more and more services and benefits for men who choose these roles, including paternity leave and change tables in men's washrooms. 20 years ago, this was unheard of, even frowned upon. Today, these have become perfectly acceptable roles for men. Men tend to be affected by the most important female authority figure in his life - his mother.

Mothers in society do everything. They solve problems, they take care of things, make purchases and make decisions.

A man's mother becomes one of the most important influences in his life, and over the years, the role of the female as head authority figure has become almost infinite. So, with 50% of marriages ending in divorce, it means at least, 50% of the men will be influenced, and probably need a strong female authority for life. Since these desires don't seem to diminish, it means the desire for a partner or spouse to be that female authority figure for a man, becomes more crucial. Men may not express it. You may not even be aware of how much family circumstances have affected your man, but what is certain is that there is a strong possibility he was raised in a single parent household, and is craving a female power figure. We women, can fulfil this role for him, and build a stronger more lasting relationships.

One theory is that as a man matures, his sexual desires become intertwined with life. His life experience becomes strongly related to his sexual fantasies. If he is used to strong female figures taking care of him, then, when he begins to enter puberty, his sexual fantasies often involve being the helpless sexual victim to one of his adult female authority figures, like an older woman, a teacher or a babysitter. Not all boys start out their sexual exploration with these types of fantasies, but many do. When these boys grow up to be men with submissive desires, they often still maintain the fantasy of being an innocent and helpless boy, that is being dominated or sexually used by an adult female authority figure. They recall that their first submissive desires were toward an older female friend of the family, a teacher, a babysitter, and they remember how pleasurable and exciting it was to have these desires. Young boys also want to please their mothers, or make them proud of their accomplishments, at school or in sports. Usually, as they become more obsessed with Adult magazines or videos, the stories and scenes where an older woman dominates a young male creates in them, the most intense sexual arousal. It is important to understand how your man responds to female authority, and what could have been the influences in his life. Don't try to force these explanations from him, because men can be very guarded about these deep, personal, early experiences.

Do you ever wonder what your man thinks as he gazes at you? Have you imagined what is going through his brain that makes him obey when you're giving him commands like "run my bath" "bring me my tea" or "make love to me now" and he does them? A man's brain is a marvelous thing. It gives him a large perspective of the world, providing him with bits of information that will help him survive and thrive in it. It also helps him figure out how to please you;, his superior female authority. Men are motivated to please women. They know instinctively, that women are of the utmost importance to their happiness and survival as a species; they have an innate understanding that they can get almost any need satisfied if they rely on a female and as a result, a man would do just about anything to get the attention and eventual affection of a woman he desires. This inherent desire to satisfy and to please is built so deep in a man's makeup that his brain is physically designed to fulfill this. To create a simple picture, imagine that a man's brain is like a superhighway of sensory information. His responses to these signals have been predetermined by the wiring of their genetic makeup. However, this doesn't mean that a man will react in the same way to the same stimuli.

The Anatomy of a Man's brain

The anatomy of the male brain is similar to that of the female's of course, as we are all humans. The cerebrum controls learning, emotions, and behavior; it also controls the muscles. The medulla oblongata controls involuntary action, and conditioned reflex actions. The brain stem, which is attached to the base of the medulla oblongata, connects stem that connects to the spinal cord; this controls the central and peripheral nervous system.

Another network in the brain, called the limbic system, is thought to be the area that controls general memory functions. While Females generally have more use of their cerebrum, men, it has been discovered, are controlled to a very large extent, by their limbic system. The medulla oblongata, which controls 'conditioned' reflex actions, is the point of importance to every female seeking to train her man to complete 100% obedience. When a child first learns to walk, it is a gradually learned process. This training, however, is saved in the brain in such a way that even several kinds of severe brain damages cannot make him forget it; it becomes a learned instinct. This is the point we want our men to get to, during training.

Instincts and Training

Sometimes, there is a natural conflict between what a man "instinctively" wants to do, and what we want him to do. This tug- of-war plays out in the limbic system of a man's brain. Most male training methods focus on overriding the natural limbic system, either by giving rewards for obeying us and ignoring instincts, or by punishing men for following instinctual tendencies.

Most male training today, is focused on these two schools of thought: rewards-based or punishment-based learning. I have used techniques from both training methods in my work, and always recommend using the methods that work best for you and your man. Rather than follow one particular method or formula, I always try to tailor my approach based on the unique man in front of me. Training is about applying a technique. This book will cover most of the techniques females are using to train men commonly used today, such as 'penalty-based' training and 'reward-based' sexual training. As a general principle, I prefer not to use the penalty-based technique in my practice, but occasionally, I have to resort to it overall; I prefer positive reward-based re-inforcement.

Work With His Instincts, Not Against Them

Many problems arise when you are unaware that men are grappling with their own feelings and emotions, which they are trained to keep hidden and guarded. Often, we are unaware that there is a problem because men fail to communicate, because it is not their strength. The key is to re-channel a man's natural energy and instincts to a behavior that is positive, for both the woman and the man. Re- direction, instead of suppression, is one of my cardinal rules. I always try to nurture and cultivate all the special skills of each specific man, harnessing these natural tendencies, and channeling them towards healthy activities. For example, I receive lots of calls from women, complaining that their men were wasting time around the house, not helping with any chores. I advise these women to tailor the tasks they give their men towards his natural instinct, rather than try to force or coerce them to go against it. Forcing a man to do something, especially a man who has already become submissive and attuned to you, would just make him unbalanced. Rather than fight the man's natural instincts, why not try creating a space where it's acceptable for the man to do what he enjoys doing?

In cavemen days, men were the hunters. This natural desire is still here. Hunting is a form of exercise, and works off excess energy.

The ability to work with the man's natural instincts may be an easier solution. Hunting is not meant to be literal. It has to be an activity engineered towards competition. Allow him to figure out the best way to accomplish a task, and give him the freedom to do it without nagging and complaining. An example would be for you to say, "Honey, I have no idea how this closet should be organized. What do you think is the best way to do it? Can you please help me with it?" You are still in control, leading by laying out the tasks, but you are giving him the freedom to complete it how he wishes.

Create special areas, where men can exercise their natural instincts. If you have a swimming pool and a man who loves the water, allow them to swim as their fitness training, or clean the pool as a chore, to help out around the house. You can also have lots of things around a house that need to be organized or constructed. Men are generally left brain dominated; so they love to organize and take action. Don't ask him to pick out the best drapes, or to choose the best color for your furniture.

I remember a submissive man, Alex, who was so tense and easily excitable that his Queen Mother was giving up on him. I could tell that Alex was anxiety ridden; he just kept looking nervous, wringing his hands as though he was missing doing something productive. After one look, I could tell that in his current state of mind, Alex would never be able to exist on a female-led relationship because my mere glance caused him to look nervous. So, I tried a different tactic. I kept him busy by taking him to a messy area of my garage and left him alone for a little, while without any explicit instructions. When I came back ten minutes later, the garage was clean and properly arranged. I don't think I have witnessed a faster transformation, ever. Not just in my garage, but also in Alex. With his instinctual needs fulfilled, he relaxed, and went into a calm, submissive state. Ever noticed a man in a kitchen who hates it? He becomes immediately petrified and confused. But give him the task to try to fix a toaster that is not working or get the air-conditioner working or organize his man-cave, he'll spend hours doing it.

According to psychologists, organizing is instinctual men. When they're working, they feel like they have a purpose in life. Allowing men to work helps boost their self-confidence, while relieving anxiety and aggression. In one relationship, I watched as the woman introduced her man to her messy master bedroom closet. The woman let the man "find his instincts." Within minutes, the man, Bill, was instinctively trying to rearrange everything in a way that made sense to him. After organizing the closet, Bill proudly walked back to his woman, and told her what he had done. She went with him to look at the closet, and she complimented him on organizing her closet so well. They sat on their bed, quietly and obediently, for a minute and then, he smiled and began massaging her feet. By allowing him to organize the closet, Bill's anxious and nervous behavior stopped.

So, his wife began to introduce him into other ways of helping around the house, and she had successfully trained him to happily perform many chores. She then redirected his energy after completing household chores into other activities that she enjoyed, like foot massages and cunnilingus and finally, she rewarded him sexually with his own orgasm. He was obedient and happy. Her job was done!

In certain cases, you may want to do the opposite of nurturing a male-specific trait. With certain powerful breeds like athletes, military men, and extreme sport enthusiasts, you may not want to encourage the particular activity that the man was originally genetically engineered to perform, like combat or fighting. You'll need to find creative ways to redirect these tendencies.

For example, my boyfriend, Michael, loves to work out, and he loves martial arts. Michael's instinct draws him to exercise and fighting. So, we play rough in the bedroom; I re-channeled the energy to a sex game, where he is gladiator and I am the Queen Mother he seduces at the Coliseum in Rome. Repression of natural, instinctual tendencies can lead to serious behavior problems; so it's better to figure out how to support the natural tendencies of your male. Fortunately, after years of being in the fitness industry, I'm in great shape, and I can keep up with him as we have long sexual sessions that get very physical and passionate. I realized the importance of exploring your man's needs, while guiding him at fulfilling ours. Women are very good at sizing up a situation and being critical. It's our nature. Good or bad, we do it, with our friend's co-workers, the movies or books we love, our children and our man. We speak what is on our minds. Men are the opposite. So, he communicates by doing things. A very basic example we hate if we are with our men, is when they look at another very attractive woman. I was in a relationship where I would chastise my boyfriend at the time, every time his eyeball began to move in the direction of an attractive female. It became such a problem; he never wanted to go out with me, and he tried so hard to stare straight ahead, that is eyes were watering with the stress and the fear that I would erupt. This is normal, and I can laugh at it now; but at the time, I know it was a great source of stress. We cannot burn out a guy's eyes with our thought if he looks at an attractive woman. It's not meant to be a criticism of us. I tell women who have this tendency to try to suppress this basic nature of men. Compare it to when women go shoe shopping. We are looking at other shoes we won't always buy, but we certainly look.

Does it mean we don't like the shoes in our closet ? No! It just means we are window shopping. To suppress that natural urge in women to stop window shopping would kill us. So, don't suppress your man's natural's urges. Re-direct the energy and attention. If you feel insecure about how you look, and you think your man would much rather be looking at others, then wear something sexy out of the blue. I'm always amazed at the reaction I get, when my man comes home to me and I am not in a t-shirt and shorts. I'm actually wearing a sexy dress with make-up on, and my nails done, for no apparent reason. Out of the blue. Now, see the reaction. Now, he's wondering and he's staring, and you feel empowered and beautiful.

On the other side, Alex was just one example of a man who experienced shutdown, when the woman in his life tried to exert too much control over him. I watched as his wife would comment on his clothes, on his job, how he did something and everything. Alex became very withdrawn and introverted. In an attempt to get away from his wife, he would lock himself in his man cave, for hours. His wife was baffled and a little hurt, because she had no idea what her behavior was doing to him. Nether Alex nor his wife was happy, and because she was strong, they believed they were involved in a Female Led Relationship. Something similar occurs when she yells at her male child too many times, and he just becomes unresponsive and sullen. When a woman is the leader and nurturer, we must allow men the freedom to make decisions in their own lives without constant interference. We are merely there to guide and allow them to serve us. Our tendency is to analyze, and try to correct everything our man, does, says, wears and believes. However, in the Female Led Relationship, we allow our men to decide how they will best serve us. This ensures his full participation, rather than bullying him into making him do what we want him to do. Full participation of both women and men in the Female Led Relationship, is what determines the success. Men need to be able to make their decisions, then focus their energy on what will satisfy both their women, and their own needs. The Female Led Relationship is not one-sided. That's the difference between Female Led and Fem Dom world of BDSM. In Female Led, the woman takes the lead, but the man has the freedom to serve his woman, in his own unique way. In BDSM, the woman exerts physical and mental control of the man, with the aim to render the man completely powerless and weak. Female led is about female empowerment, and the man is also empowered to make his own decisions about the relationship. It's a union of love, not pain and humiliation. Neither the man nor the woman is powerless, and this is why it works. In a Female Led Relationship, women are leading and setting ground rules, but the man is doing what he does best, providing for, protecting and serving his "Queen", his woman.

What a Man Remembers

Now that you have a basic understanding of how a man's brain works, and how he processes sensory inputs, it's equally important to understand how his memory recall works. Let's face it ladies; men don't remember every aspect of the relationship like we do. Their ability to mainly "live in the moment" is what makes them so trainable, but it can hamper their thought process. In my two decades of working with hundreds of men, there has only been a handful that I failed to help. While scientific research on how men perceive time and recall events is limited, about memory and time, we know men are different from women. My experience has taught me that men cannot mentally travel back in time or into the future, as quickly or as well as females do. To be able to recall specific memories and anticipate events, in the future, seems like a beautiful gift, but at the same time, these female abilities come with a cost: anxiety, dread, guilt, and regret.

Many of my clients are skeptical when I tell them men live mainly in the present, and that their real memory span is very short—about 30 seconds. "After all, they argue," my man is trained to massage my feet every time I ask. They do remember what to do. But that's not what is happening in their brains. Remember, men have learned how to react to commands, and to please females. So, men can know how to respond to the command, without having a memory of the particular event where you taught it to them.

A man remembers women and places based on associations he has had with both. Associative memory can work, both positively and negatively. If a man has a traumatic memory about being dumped in his past love life, he may react with fear, until that memory association is replaced by a new happier memory. The stronger the connection, the harder it is to replace. When psychologists worked with traumatized men, they must first identify their negative associations. It takes time and patience to rewire these associations. It is the same when you attempt to introduce new rules and commands for behavior to your man. Be aware that he may not respond at first because of past negative events, but the more you can work daily and re-enforce the good behavior with rewards, the more he will respond to you. I see a complete change in my man when I compliment him, touch his muscles or caress him just for fun. It's his reward. The more you do it, the more you reward him, the better his behavior. I purposely compliment my man everyday, and this has gone a long way to inspiring him, because I think it goes to a basic human need that we all need someone to believe in us. So, as the leader in the relationship, I recognize that a man wants to serve his woman, but he still requires encouragement and recognition. Sometimes, our busy lives can get in the way of a simple compliment, but I have seen first hand, how this can change everything.

So, if your man spends the whole day organizing the garage, you will get a much better response if you reward him with positive compliments, and a nice dinner, rather than criticism. He has still fulfilled his end of the Female Led Relationship, because he did what you asked of him. This is particularly important with men in the military. When they leave, they may still be affected by negative experiences. So, loud noises or yelling orders, arguing, or any kind of aggressive behavior can send them into a tailspin. It's important to be gentle, loving and patient; really enhancing the positive experiences in your relationship, to prevent negative triggers.

Stimulate the Brain, Early and Often

A question that I get often is, "How can I make my man better mentally?" If you look online and in stores, you'll see numerous supplements which claim to aid in intelligence. Everyone desires to be mentally strong, so, having this desire for your man is nothing new. A man who is mentally and physically strong, only serves you and your family better.

To begin, I recommend the basics - good nutrition, exercise, stress management, and good sleep. However, I add adequate stimulation everyday, so that you have his attention, and he is challenged to work on the relationship to continue to please you. Balancing his stresses with his sexual urges, work, and play, are all necessary to create a stronger, more balanced male brain. A man's brain is like a sponge— soaking up all the sounds, smells, sights and experiences in the world, as fast as it can. A well-stimulated man will have a larger brain with more cells, bigger cells, and more interconnections between them. Getting regular exercise, being well trained by his Queen, traveling to new places, and even going through specific sexual training for a few minutes each day, makes for a better gentleman. We can influence the development of a man's brain by providing him with the best environment possible, right from the beginning of his reconditioning, under your care. But this takes daily attention on your part. We all need a coach; so in many ways, you will be his coach, cheerleader and partner. You must not only set aside the time and the energy to devote a few minutes each day to his training, you must also lead by example, and take care of your own mental and physical health. A man respects his Queen, who also takes very good care of herself, and is an example to him and your family. This constant daily attention is what becomes challenging on the Female-Led Relationship, but you will be rewarded with a man who is more attentive, interested and present.

A man, who isn't properly stimulated or doesn't have interactions with others, will be less balanced. Don't let your man isolate himself, and spend hours alone in his man-cave. This does nothing to improve your relationship. I have witnessed, first-hand, how many men, when left under-stimulated by their partner, is very unhappy, dull and withdrawn. On the flipside, too much of a good thing can be harmful. Allowing your man to party and hang with friends too often, engage in aggressive behavior or sports, or spend lots of time without you, also lead to destructive habits. Unfortunately, I saw this happen first hand with the break up of my own parents' marriage, which I attribute to my mother's inability to control my father's constant need for attention, spending almost everyday of the week socializing, drinking and away from home. Sometimes, it's impossible to break these habits, but a strong relationship is never built on spending almost no time together. Men and women are guilty of this, believing that their partner needs to de-stress or for simplicity sake, they allow habits like this to continue. However, in my experience of working with many couples, constant over-stimulation and time spent apart leads to the destruction of the cohesive bond between two people. A balance must be struck with activities alone, and outside of the house.

Sometimes, over stimulation can occur when a man is allowed to spiral out of control with aggressive behavior. I was once in a relationship myself, where my partner would scream at people at the top of his lungs, and throw things when he was angry. I was very young, and I thought it was just a sign of manliness; so I allowed it to happen. But soon, I found myself copying this behavior until the aggression spiraled out of control, and I could no longer tolerate it.

The aggression was not the only problem in the relationship, but it created less and less opportunities for constructive work on the relationship and eventually, it was one of the major factors which led to us growing apart and the end of it. Signs of over-stimulation can be recognized in a man who enters a room or approaches another man face-to-face, with aggressive behavior, puffing up his chest, and even insulting or yelling. A lot of male leaders misinterpret these signs as those of a "strong" man, but in reality, such men are out of control.

When you see these signs, your man needs calm, deliberate handling, and it's best to move him away from whatever is over stimulating him, until he has calmed down. Encourage him to be around positive people; friends or relatives, who can influence him in a positive way. It is not wise to ever encourage violence or disobedience. In the Female Led Relationship, when a man is out of control, if you have trained him well, he will submit to you as his Queen and leader. But, you must be respectful in the way you issue the command, and be careful not to antagonize the situation. I see this mistake made early on, in attempting to follow the female-led lifestyle. In our effort to assume control, we will engage in argumentative or condescending behavior towards our man. This is the opposite of how you control him if he is spiraling out of control. You gently remind him of how to behave, and show him he is behaving improperly. I use the analogy of when you try to train a child. By yelling at him or her constantly, he or she learns to ignore you. However, I have seen much better behavior come from positive reinforcement, where the child is shown the error and rewarded when the correct behavior occurs. When your man corrects his aggressive behavior, you must reward him.

Draw him a bath, invite him in with you, give him a massage, or initiate sex. It is important to always reward the good behavior, so he is gently under your guidance. We all remember times when our parents yelled at us, but most of those instances never result in positive changes. We also can recall when we were motivated to do better because they rewarded us. This is ingrained in the human being, and your man will respond.

If my man becomes disrespectful at any moment, I immediately remind him, that the queen is not happy with his response, and that he needs to change it. That generally diffuses any arguments, and makes for a much happier relationship. Many times, men will recognize their bad behavior, and will change if you disapprove.

You correct the behavior, and not criticize the man. It's a much netter way to deal with your man who may be overstimulated.

Be as attentive as you can, and listen constructively to your man when he attempts to voice concerns or thoughts. Men generally will never tell you what is bothering them. You need to decipher it from listening intently, to when they do speak and their behavior. This is where we, women must step into the leadership position and take charge of the relationship. Part of being a great leader is to identify when there are challenges ahead. A man will always signal there is a problem, but they are not master communicators. So, you need to be tuned, and ready to listen and take action, should he voice concerns. A man may say, "I love when you wear that dress." You may be tempted to think, "My butt's too big in that dress" and dismiss his comment. But, the fact is, he has indicated he is turned on and attracted to you, when you wear that dress; so, he really means, "please wear that dress more often." A nice reward for your man is for you to wear the dress. As women, we take a man's comments of what we wear or how we look as criticisms because of our own insecurities. But, I remind couples, you are not here to please the world, other women or men. So, if you are constantly worried about what strangers think of your appearance, career and activities, and you ignore your partner, that's where the problem begins. Couples must perform a check to make sure they are both on a common track. So, it is super important to take note of what he is saying to you. If your man is voicing his opinions and thoughts, take them seriously.

When it comes to the subjects of human sexuality, female domination and male submissive desires, what I have learned is that there are reasons why men have these desires, and a person's core nature expresses itself in the sexual realm, through different sexual desires. It is important to understand why your man may need certain things, and you must refrain from criticizing. Part of being in the driver's seat is to anticipate what your man needs, and try to fulfill his desires while he fulfills yours. It does not mean you ignore what he wants, while he gives you what you want. He must be made to feel special if he is to respond to your wishes. I base most of this advice on researching Female Led Relationships and male submission for over 15 years, counseling many submissive men and female led couples, and interviewing many couples that practice this lifestyle. I have also personally lived this lifestyle, and I still actively practice this way of life. It is important to note that Female Led Relationships have nothing to do with BDSM or Fem Dom community.

The idea of beating, tying up, or having a man crawl around like a baby, is not a Female Led Relationship. The two could not be more different. This is very important because, it is a perversion that the media tends to want to inflate, and link it to women in power. In BDSM, the female is not in leadership role because she is actually responding to man's desire to be humiliated. It is entertainment and a perversion. In the Female Led Relationship, the man is loved and served as much as he serves. The difference is that the female leads, and the submissive man is happy to serve her in whatever way he chooses, nothing to do with humiliation and perversion of BDSM. In a Female Led Relationship, women are in charge. It is the same as prostitutes. Some women believe that they have power because they get paid, and they give men what they want. But a prostitute is not a woman in power. As soon as a man has to pay you, he calls the shots. Whether you beat him, tie him up, have sex or are in a threesome, he pays and you do. There is no power there. So, a dominatrix can seem as though she has power, but really, she can only act in a position of power because she's being paid to do so. This is the furthest thing from a woman, who takes charge in her relationship, and leads a loving relationship of mutual respect. I am always intrigued by the movie, "50 shades of Grey". On the surface, it looks like Christian Grey, the main character, calls the shots and has control. But, in the end, he can't function without his muse. So, he is not in control once money is involved, and neither is she. This movie had much acclaim, because women have a secret desire to be tied up and controlled by their men sexually but, in fact, there is no power plays at all in this movie. Anatassia is a slave, and Christian pays her to be just that. But he is lost without his ability to pay her and have her do what he wants. So in essence, there is no power at all in the relationship. But the movie is very good at hiding this important point, with all the grandeur of a lavished lifestyle. I actually have a good chuckle when Anatassia becomes so angry when Christian wants to whip her, yet she succumbs to his contract, and agrees to be paid. It is important to distinguish perversion from power.

Actually, the Female Led Relationship is not something new. Females have always been revered as the nurturing, loving and the life giving force of humanity in the universe, and the continuous cycle of birth, death and regeneration is made possible by women. The matriarchal view of the world is one of sublime grandeur, where women inspire chivalry, chastity, and poetry in men. Although men may have superior strength,

44

women strive for peace, justice, and religious consecration, and work to guide man's wild, lawless and primitive beast-like nature. Female led relationships are unique because, most of our institutions are patriarchal. Society is evolving, and the empowerment of women is not isolated from the desire of men wanting to submit to women, both sexually and socially.

Keeping Your Relationship Alive

We all know how easy it is to start a relationship, but how difficult it is to keep the spice alive. Relationships take work, daily. Being with the same person, day in and day out, can seem to get boring. A training program for your man, naturally addresses boredom. Like any other worthwhile project, goals and mini milestones are one way to keep both you and your man focused on the success of the relationship, rather than allowing it to fall apart. Just like you must tend to a garden every day to keep it manicured and beautiful, it's the same with relationships. Daily attention helps to prevent the "weeds" or disconnect from creeping in, and setting mini goals can help to keep you both, moving forward. This is particularly important if you have children, and many other responsibilities. It's easy for relationship issues to get swept under the rug and forgotten, until they begin. One of you gets bored or begins to lose interest. If it is a man undergoing your training, or maybe a trained one, this could disrupt all the progress you both have made. Here, I've included a couple of tips that could help add spice to your relationship:

1. Teach him new tricks.

When your man knows your body too well, it can lead to one of two things; the first is that he understands how to bring you pleasure always in the same way, the second is boredom sets in. He may begin to let things slide, and being together might become monotonous. Show him how to rediscover your body, come up with interesting new ways to serve you better. A very good example is the character of "Samantha" on the show "Sex In the City"-She was always engaging in sex with multiple partners, but even when she had a steady boyfriend, she understood the importance of changing it up. So, I remember a couple of interesting episodes, where she and her steady hunk boyfriend played detective and spy, or French maid, and added whipped cream to bedroom activities. I support the idea of changing it up as much as you can. Change the times, the positions, the locations. Add costumes, role play and surprises. You would be surprised that even though it may seem like a stupid thought, the action of changing it up, with we, women, initiating sex more often, goes a long way to keeping the spice alive. I have consulted many couples in 30+ year marriages, and I'm always amazed at all of the ideas they offer but, the one which stands out, is to switch it up to prevent boredom. I can recall one of my own friends informing me that she had to skip our exercise class, which we always did together on a Wednesday night, because her husband of 32 years was traveling and coming home, and she needed to do her duty.

And she said it with a mischievous smile on her face. I was stunned at the time, because they were a couple in their 50's, married for more than 30 years, still having fun in their sex life.

2. Play games and use toys.

Sex toys have evolved beyond rubber dildos and ball gags. Develop games that encourage him to think. I like to create puzzles that allow you to hide "Sexual Reward Notes" around the house, perhaps where your man works on his "guy things", which engages your man to try and find them. Another version of the game; you can hold a "Sexual Reward Note" in one hand, and let your man figure out which hand is hiding the note. Or agree to try a new sex toy each month. One night, I returned home and waiting for me on the table, was a present, all wrapped up. The game that night was me blindfolded, and opening the present, trying to figure out what it does and how to use it during sex, without seeing it. It's always fun and interesting for both you and your man to try new things in a very safe environment. For some time, I would switch up the times for love-making, and pull out a surprise at 3AM in the morning. Though it was a sleepless night, we both got through the next day in euphoria, because we had such a fun night. It lightened things up, and kept the relationship interesting.

3. Change your sex routine.

One of the easiest ways to have fun is to sneak downstairs in the basement, or have sex in your pool, for a change. During your kids sleepover, have a night of pleasure, in your living room or in the kitchen. Couples have reported to me that they cook dinner together, just wearing only an apron, and that enhanced the excitement. We are always so worried about our partners seeing us naked, but there is not a man in the world who has not seen his partner's cellulite or heavy thighs. I encourage developing little names for it. Like "dimple butt" or "Thunder from down under". If you are light about it, he will love you more because you are confident in your own skin, and the fact that you love each other unconditionally, builds confidence. Acceptance of your body is a very important step in empowerment. Women, who are comfortable in their own skin, will be comfortable leading the relationship, because it takes great strength and power to hold yourself in the position of "Queen" and love yourself.

4. Give your man a job to do.

We have established that men are bred to complete tasks, like organizing and fixing things. So, let him set the scene for sex. Let him add his favorite things to do. Explore his fantasies openly, with him. Many women report that men have fantasies to be with a celebrity or another woman. So, my suggestion was, if he likes Wonder Woman, get a costume, surprise him in it, or put on a wig, do something to engage in his fantasy with him. Pretty soon, he's going forget all about it, and just enjoy you trying. When men can engage in their fantasies with you, they are less likely to be going anywhere else to engage in them.

5. Allow him to socialize.

Men are social animals, and you should nurture the need for social activity by allowing him outings with other compatible and trained men. Guys night out is very important for a man. He must engage with other men to feed the masculine part of him, and this is important. Socially, a man is balanced when he can engage with others, and as I mentioned previously, a man who is withdrawn and isolated will never be able to be present enough in your relationship. So, allow him time to socialize enough, but not too much. He still needs to attend to your needs as well. Social events should never take the place of your times together.

6. See Things Your Man's Way.

Most of the happiest, most balanced men that I have interacted with seem to have Female Leaders, who instinctively understand them. They can understand the world their men live in, and help guide them through it. You can become that kind of Female Relationship Leader, too. That is why it's so vital to understand how your man's brain works, how it processes information, and how instincts can drive behavior. By having a firm grasp on all this information, you're well equipped to move on to the following chapters that build on this foundation. Being able to "see" your man's unique point of view will help you embrace the techniques and principles to come.

CHAPTER THREE

--—⊱✖⊰—--

The Natural Man Laws

A very popular question is, "What exactly is male's Psychology?"

Many believe that a man's psychology is the same as that of a female's, but it isn't. Females are genetically wired to teach, to nurture, to love, to guide, and provide care for others. Males are genetically wired to seek the love training, the nurturing, the loving, the guidance and the care, from his female authority figure. Many of us tend to forget this fact and then, try to turn our loving men into shadows of ourselves. Masculine psychology is based on this unique perspective of how a man sees women, his thoughts, feelings and emotions, toward female authority. We need to build a healthy environment for him to feel comfortable and free to explore his desire to serve you as a Queen, without any hindrance from criticism or over-analysis.

Now, it's time to find out how to harness this desire and bring it out, so that he can have the female authority he seeks, and at the same time, bring out the best in him. To better examine this psychology and genetic science, I've developed a couple of guidelines I like to call my Natural Man Laws. If you are going to control your man and be his leader, you must understand who men are, and what they need as men.

What are these Natural Man Laws?

At their core, they are the end results of thousands of years of evolution, from cave men to modern men. In modern men, with so many being raised by single mothers or "mostly absent" fathers, the view of the female as the authority figure is greater than ever, now. This social change to more female led households is a driving force of the total transition of future society to a matriarchal society run by women. The revolution to a female led world is happening, one household at a time. There are fundamental truths that must be understood, for both sexes to live together in harmony. These powerful forces still continue to shape how modern men think and behave. These are the laws that Mother Nature and every man's Mother have placed upon the species, and that our environment has fine tuned. You are his adult female authority. When ignored or suppressed, the outcome is an all-round unbalanced and unhappy man. Sigmund Freud's famous psychoanalytic theory, the Oedipus complex, is based on a desire for sexual involvement with the parent of the opposite sex, and a sense of rivalry with the parent of the same sex. The term derives from the Theban hero Oedipus of Greek legend, who unknowingly slew his father and married his mother. This deep rooted subconscious desire to be loved by the mother drives men into adulthood as well. All men secretly crave to replace the loving female authority of a Mother figure with an adult female authority figure. It is not a sick desire; it is a natural desire to love and have undying gratitude to the female gender that gives all men life, gives our species life, and raises all men from infancy to adulthood.

The Five Natural Laws of a Man's Psychology are:

1. He deeply wants you to love him for himself, and not just for what he can do for you.

2. He wants you to be his leader, his mother figure, and have a high opinion of yourself.

3. He wants you to believe in his ability to communicate his true feelings to you.

4. He wants you to be sexually playful, and allow him to fulfill his need to serve you and bring you pleasure.

5. He wants you to know that men are sensitive, and they do cry, and they need you to comfort them.

6. It's important to understand these laws, as they will affect how you relate to your man, especially during challenging times. An example is when he refuses to do something you ask. I have been asked so many times by women, "Why won't my man do what I say?" The simple answer is that men are stubborn, and they like working things out their way. Often, a man may refuse to do what you ask simply because he is set in his ways and refuses to change. What you must do as his female leader, is to approach it with kindness and understanding, rather than complaining and arguing. Impress upon him, how

important this is to you, and how much you would love to reward him for doing what you've asked. Then he will be much more motivated to do it without question, and you are building the habit.

Research suggests that men, who feel they must wholeheartedly conform to masculine gender norms, are more likely to suppress emotions that make them feel vulnerable. These are the very emotions required for emotional intimacy with a romantic partner. However, refrain from simply dismissing your man, because he may show this behavior. You can still work with him and bring him around under your control by understanding the natural laws.

The First Natural Man Law:

He deeply wants you to love him for himself and not just for what he can do for you.

Male socialization teaches them that their value is in their ability to take charge, to be in control, and to win. Do not let this facade mislead you to think that he doesn't want you to take charge and be in control. Underneath this male bravado, is a child, who wants to feel loved by his female authority figure for who he is. He wants "mommy" to love him even if he gets a "c" on his test at school. He wants you to love him, even if he's not a winner or the richest guy or the best athlete. Unlike women, men have more difficulty talking about emotions related to their weaknesses, so when he is not feeling good enough, you may not even know it. This is why men desire a female authority, who will love them for simply being "their loving and obedient" male companion. If you keep this key in mind, you will have an easier time controlling your man. Let him know that you enjoy spending time with him and his sense of humor, or just talking with him about your life together. Tell him that you love him because he is a gentleman, and treats you like a Queen. The more a man can feel that you love him for who he is, the more he will comply with your wishes.

The Second Natural Man Law:

He wants you to be his leader, his mother figure and have a high opinion of yourself.

When you accept yourself as a Queen, your man will look up to you and be inspired by you. He will want to do everything possible, to keep you on a pedestal, once you can show him you really are his Queen. He will want to bask in your admiration of him, and he will be inspired to serve you the best he can. Projection is the tendency to project characteristics that we find desirable onto others.

In other words, if you are happy with yourself, you will compliment him for being such a gentleman and such a "good boy", and this will motivate him to be even better behaved. When you criticize your man constantly, you are triggering Kryptonite in him, and it will make him feel endlessly nagged and deflated. A man who is deflated can't get much done, and he can sink into depression. When you are constantly criticizing, men acquire a sense that they can 'never get it right.' They feel defeated, and everything starts to feel dull and pointless. I truly believe that most men would sit on the couch in their underwear and drink beer, like many bachelors, if they did not have a wife and family to motivate them to provide. If your man feels like he can't please you, this is very damaging to your relationship, and can lead to him retrieving into himself, and acting distant and withdrawn. A man cannot handle being constantly criticized. I believe that it triggers feelings of being disciplined by his mother in childhood. Women can tend to unconsciously treat their men like children, particularly if they must deal with many challenges at home.

But when you trigger this horrible experience from childhood in your man, he can either become withdrawn, or become aggressive. Either way, it is not healthy, and will lead to a communication breakdown. Gentle reminders and simple corrections, can go a long way to restoring the peace. Conversely, if you constantly praise him for being such a gentleman and treating you so well, he will be more attentive and want to be around you as much as possible, waiting on your every need to receive more praise and sexual rewards.

This is another reason why I disagree wholeheartedly with the dark BDSM community and their desire to feminize men; let your man be a proud, loving masculine man, and he will obey and serve you better than you ever dreamed possible.

1. Don't enforce your feminine ways of life on him.

2. Don't attribute female feelings and emotions to your man's actions, body language, or facial expressions. Don't make him feel like a "sissy."

3. Don't make a man dress-up in a feminine way with flowered shirts or wearing bright colors if he is not into it. Some men love to get dressed up and be stylish, but the idea is not to force him.

4. Don't expect your man to understand and interpret your behavior. Men cannot read your body language, nor decipher moods.

5. Don't apply female solutions to male problems. Try to see it from the "Natural Man Rules" point-of-view that you are learning here.

The Third Natural Man Law:

He wants you to believe in his ability to communicate his true feelings to you.

Although men may not be able to communicate their emotional feelings and shortcomings as well as women, men actually can communicate. You need to create a comfortable environment for your man to open up and communicate with you. The most important point is you need to treat him with respect, in regard to his ability to talk about his feelings and what motivates him to be your perfect gentleman. Once he opens up to communicate his most vulnerable thoughts and emotions, he will try harder and harder to communicate and please you in your conversations. Give your man a chance to open up and communicate, and this only enhances your role as his female authority figure. Listen to him and talk to him the way a kind and loving mother would listen to her son express himself at an emotional childhood moment. Yes, women are more verbal—they typically talk about their feelings more quickly and succinctly, than men. But men do know what they think and feel. Instead of shaming him, when he is trying to express something vulnerable, take him seriously, ask questions and show him how proud you are by rewarding him sexually for his openness - even if it's just a loving kiss. Make sure you thank him for sharing and talking to you on this deep level. Trust me, if you do this, he will talk more, and you will see that under his tough manly exterior, there is a sensitive gentleman who will learn to speak more articulately, and share his feelings more often than you can imagine. This new open communication will make you his loving female authority figure, and allows you to lead your relationship without tension or friction and "the silent treatment" on either side of the fence.

The Fourth Natural Man Law:

He wants you to be sexually playful and allow him to fulfill his need to serve you and bring you pleasure.

You are your man's lover, above all else. This may be a difficult concept to grasp. Sure your man appreciates that you are a good mother, a good friend and partner but, above all, you are his sexual partner. Only you can enhance his sexual experience. I believe this is another point of disconnection, especially when everyone is stressed from long hours at work and chores to be done, and household duties need to be completed, getting into a sexy mood, takes work. I found that the best way to approach this was to do something to arouse my partner every time I was around him. I would give him a compliment or slap his butt, or do something playful, that was aimed at being more sexual. I found that this was able to alleviate any feelings of disconnection or even bad moods, especially during times of stress. When you remember that both you and your man are sexual beings, this is a part of the relationship that cannot be brushed aside. How he views you will go a long way to helping you to create the right environment for a loving Female Led Relationship. Strong women are pro at organization, multitasking, and 'taking care of business', but this can go overboard, especially if your man is trying to fulfill the subservient role.

You are not inspiring him by nagging him as a means of trying to motivate him. Some strong dominant women will feel that they have to do it to "light a fire under him" but, this could only result in driving him further into himself. Being dominant but sexy, is a different story. You could easily put your man in good mood if you can combine your leadership with being playful and sexy. He wants to see you let go of control, and be spontaneous and sexual, in the moment with him. Think Cleopatra, who could bring Ceasar to his knees with one look.

The Fifth Natural Man Law:

He wants you to know that men are sensitive and they do cry and they need you to comfort them.

Deep down, just like you, men are sensitive and vulnerable human beings. Praise and reward him, hug him; if you see even a hint of sadness, let him have his moment. Men are typically socialized to cry less than women. So, if he is sad, he may or may not cry, but certainly, if he is even close, hug him and tell him you love him, and that it's okay to let it out. It is important for his unhappy emotions to be released and expressed. Unfortunately, boys and men are often humiliated in our culture for being vulnerable. So much so that they are often left with anger and violence to vent their unhappy emotions. You are his loving Female authority, and that's why he needs you, wants you and loves you. You are the one person in the world, where he can unconditionally bring his full inner self out into the open, and you don't judge him. Let him express his fears or upsets; offer him compassion and be understanding. If a man had a loving mother, he received these two important qualities in his childhood, but even if he did not, and many men did not, remember, it's still up to you to give him that compassion and understanding in his adulthood. Remember I told you that men want a loving Female Led Relationship? So, stop, breathe and remember; deep down, most men simply want what women want; to be accepted for who they are; they want love and positive reinforcement for what they do, and appreciation for what they are trying to contribute.

I have been able to help a number of males to come to terms with their desires, and their natural submissive nature. Likewise, my knowledge of Female Led Relationships, and its social and sexual importance, helps me to share with women, why men have these desires, and how exploring these desires with them in a safe and sane environment can develop a strong bond of intimacy, between the Female and her gentleman. I share with women, how domination and submission and more specifically, Female Led Relationships, can be liberating for the woman and the man. It will cause a power exchange within their relationship, and that power exchange will be beneficial for both parties. It's what men and women naturally want. Woman is the mother of man. Man is the child, who seeks to be unconditionally loved.

Before I began counseling men and before I embraced the Female Led Relationships lifestyle, I was of the opinion that only a man with a low self-image or a man that was sexually dysfunctional would desire to be dominated by a woman.

However, after 15 years of studying and practicing this lifestyle, I have discovered that these desires are very common and natural within men. I have concluded that the number one sexual fantasy and desire among men is to be loved by a female authority figure.

Furthermore, I now understand and have shared with you, the dynamics of male psychology, about why men desire these things, where these desires originate from, and how they can fit within one's sexuality and personal relationships in a healthy, positive, and loving way.

CHAPTER FOUR

---∞---

Love & Obey Rules

Love yourself first, and everything else falls into line. You really have to love yourself to get anything done in this world.

-Lucille Ball

A happier life with your man becomes easy to achieve once you see your man as a gentleman, and honor what's unique about him. Soon, he will be excited and grateful to you that he can obey and serve your every need, and you will enjoy the many pleasures of being his Queen Mother. Now, you're truly able to appreciate the differences in the way females and males perceive and interact with the world. Armed with this knowledge, you can now move into your rightful position as the leader in your relationship. But you will need to follow some rules to create a training and de- programming, for you and your man. These key lessons are my secret weapons in creating a balance for any female Leader — whether you have lots of experience or none at all, in a Female Led Relationship. The rules also help you to sail through the days when challenges pop up, and there may be a period of disruption, until both you and your man are accustomed to relating correctly. By following the rules, you will be able to communicate verbally and instinctively, and understand each other's needs.

Love & Obey Rules #1: Be Aware of Your Mother Energy

Women have the ability to connect to their Mother energy. We know how powerful Mother Nature is, and it is the same with Mother energy in women. Energy can affect everything, and it can affect your relationship, and even your own daily behavior. You want to try to be balanced as you take your man through the training in the Female Led Relationship. Mother energy is the deep unconditional love women can have for their mate and their children. It is this energy which will be crucial for helping your man feel comfortable, expressing himself in your new Female Led Relationship. Mother energy is the highest amount of love energy that a female can give, and this will be important to show unconditional love, no matter what your man does. If he fails at first, to attend to your needs, or he becomes argumentative or angry, you still approach him with all of your Mother energy - Loving, understanding and with your whole being. Once you are in your Mother energy, you are better able to be aware of your communication - verbal and non-verbal. Your man needs lots of compliments, and loving language. Remember he needs his ego boosted, to help him feel calm and happy about transitioning into giving you the reigns to lead the relationship. You can enhance your own Mother energy with a couple minutes of re- balancing with meditation or quiet. Take time to re-center your own emotions, so your energy can be restored. You can't give what you don't have. Your man need lots of energy, along with your kids and other responsibilities, like aging parents or extended family. So get light exercise, and add mini stress management strategies, to help to re-balance your energy. Females are better communicators, so we are in a much better position to sway discussions and any disagreements. While this is not strange or wrong, we have a more advanced intellectual capacity for speech, after all, it is very easy for us to loose touch with our own Mother Nature Energy, disregarding the signals we are projecting to the world. However, because of our dependence on language, we often do pick up on each other's energy, as well as we should, and it affects how our message is perceived. Quite often, I will work with women who are unaware that they project nervous or weak energy. This can affect your man and your children, as everyone looks up to you to keep the energy positive. To be successful as the relationship leader, you need to be mindful of your Mother energy, and learn to control it, even when you aren't feeling particularly calm or assertive. Be aware of the universal energy of Mother Nature as well. We are the creators of all life, and all the creative and positive energy of the universe, flows through us. This energy is the reason men crave for women who carry themselves as Queens, because they project positive energy, which helps men to feel confident and calm in the Female Led Relationship.

Here is a quick exercise for you. Take a moment right now, and pay attention to how you're feeling emotionally; then notice how you're holding your body. Is your chest lifted up, straight back, happy smile, or do you slouch, look tired, or angry or sullen? We don't just live with ourselves, and this was a challenge; to be aware of body language, our moods, and what we project to our mate. You can go a long way towards projecting a positive energy by being aware of your posture. Think of the regal stance of a Queen, and try and maintain this at all times. Think of how a Queen carries herself, and try to carry yourself in the same manner. Stand straight, with your head up, shoulders back, and chest out. Keep both feet flat on the ground. Try to avoid crossing your arms or shoving your hands in your pockets. Inhale deeply, and exhale slowly. Stand like this for a few minutes, focus on your breathing, and try to clear your mind of random thoughts. If it is safe to do so, close your eyes and concentrate on what you can smell and hear. You should find yourself calming down naturally. If this sounds like yoga, it's because it isn't that different. Practicing yoga is a great way to make yourself aware of your natural energy, and master control over it. I would recommend women take yoga classes, to learn some basic techniques that they can apply to their role as the Queen Mother. File away this feeling and the accompanying body language, and then practice being able to switch into this state subconsciously, and on demand. In dealing with your man, it is paramount to understand the importance of projecting unstable energy. This will always be interpreted by the man as confusing and upsetting. This is why it is so important to become aware of your own energy.

Love & Obey Rules #2: Live in the Moment.

One major difference between males and females is that, we are very good multi-taskers, which means, at any given moment, we are constantly doing a number of things, at the same time. We tend to continue to do this in our relationships as well. While we are having dinner, we may be thinking about work or the children, or a list of chores we forgot to do. One of the most important things to do, when transitioning your man into a Female Led Relationship, is to encourage both of you to be in the moment. As human beings, we get into the habit of checking our phones at the dinner table, or doing work before bed, watching TV and looking at our phone, while we are having a quiet time with our mates. Refrain from this practice, as much as possible, if you want to strengthen your relationship with your man. In the beginning, there may be a great need for scheduled quiet times. During these moments, you are giving 100% of your attention to your man, and demanding the same from him. Phones are off, kids are in bed, and there are no chores going on. At this moment, while you are reading, you may be thinking about dinner, or a meeting tomorrow, or an event you have to attend. Use this time and reading this book to train your attention to be 100% on what you are doing, so this can be extended to your man. You will need to take the lead to schedule a quiet, one on one time, with him, and you may need to encourage him to take these moments seriously. This undivided attention, which you give each other, can make or break your relationship because it is the time you can re-enforce goals and important moments, in your relationship. Too often, relationships begin to suffer when we get so caught up in life's duties, that we forget our men. In a Female Led Relationship, the responsibility of one on one time, will fall squarely on your shoulders but, if you make it a weekly habit, it will go a long way to strengthening your relationship.

The one-on-one time can be used for love-making or just doing something nice, together. The idea of the date; having a date with your man and practicing your Queen position will be very beneficial in keeping your relationship strong. Men are more likely to enjoy the moment because they are not as good at multi-tasking. But it is important to ensure that you keep your man's attention on the relationship and being together in the moment, rather than thinking about work, or looking at his phone or computer. Living in the moment also means letting go of the past. Women tend to focus on men's behavior in the past. Bringing up past transgressions does not move your Female Led Relationship forward. Let go of his past mistakes, and provide loving positive re-enforcement for the future. Refrain from holding grudges. Remember, you cannot change the past; you can only accept it.

It will only be a hindrance to the success of your Female Led Relationship, if you lead while always focusing on the past. There is a famous saying, "You can't move forward looking in the rear-view mirror." He is more likely to give you the reigns completely, if you gently nudge him forward. Men, by nature, do not hold grudges, and they do not tend to dwell on the past. So, use this tendency to breathe new life, excitement and energy into your relationship, by focusing on making it stronger, together. The ability to be fully present in the "now" is a blessing for the relationship, allowing you and your man to keep moving forward.

Here is a good exercise. Pause for a second, and think of any criticisms you may have of your man. Just sit with them for a bit, then, gently allow them to be released, and replace those thoughts with the things which make you smile. What does he do to make you love him so much? Maybe it's the look, maybe it's little quirks that he has. Let them sit with you, and make you happy. This is being present, and letting go of the past. You are going to be in a much better place to lead your man in a Female Led Relationship if you are happier.

Holding on to negative moments and emotions can change the focus and the energy in your relationship. You want your man to be happy and contented to allow you to lead, and you show much of your Queen and Mother energy, by leading him in a positive direction. This does not mean, forgetting the good times you shared. Sometimes, it's nice for couples to remember some of the nice times they shared, through photos or videos. Just don't spend every moment re-living the past. It does not serve the relationship long-term.

Love & Obey Rules #3: Men Can't Hide the Truth

Men really cannot hide the truth, so they will always tell you how they are feeling. You know, sometimes, he comes home and he has an uneasy and tensed look on his face. Well, ladies, this is not the time to bring up the backyard needs to be mowed or there's a leak in the roof. As the leader in the Female Led Relationship, it will be up to you to comfort your man in times when he is down, weakened or exhausted. You must be attentive to his moods, and try your best to be comforting and uplifting.

Sometimes, it's just easier to allow him to get through his mood, with as little stress as possible. If your man is upset or pensive, allow him to be in this mood. Draw a nice bath, or cook a nice dinner for him, then you can take the lead by deciding that you're just going to relax and have a glass of wine, or watch a movie, or sit on the sofa together. If he seems like he's in an energetic mood, then suggest going out for a walk together, or go do a workout together. Sometimes, just being together is enough to give support and practice being in the driver's seat but also being aware of his feelings. Again, women tend to be able to discuss more openly about what they are thinking and feeling, but this does not happen as readily with men.

They are more guarded about their feelings, but by observing behavior and gently nudging him in conversation, you can create an atmosphere of openness, while leading.

A real life example was when I helped a young lady, who we will call Ann. She and her boyfriend, Matt (Not his real name), were at my counseling session because Ann had been complaining that Matt didn't like communicating with her. Now, from what I observed, he was a gentle, highly introverted, quiet and shy guy. Ann, instead of looking for other means of communicating her feelings, began to become clingy, in an attempt to keep him close. Matt did not like this behavior, and usually became nervous around her, and she thought he could have been cheating on her. The truth behind the situation was that Ann didn't trust Matt, and Matt knew it. Now, think for a moment, would you follow a person you knew didn't trust you? Ann was too timid, too fearful, and she was projecting that energy to her man. My reaction was simple. Ann needed to observe when Matt's behavior changed, and she had to understand what she was seeing. She needed to realize that Matt's reaction to clinginess had nothing to do with cheating. Only that, he hated Ann's reaction. So, by changing her response to Matt's natural tendency to "shell up", I was able to re-train both Ann and Matt, to understand their tendencies, and how to change the energy and the behavior so it was much more positive. Ann had to back off;

Matt was feeling constricted, and she needed to continue to create an energy of openness to allow Matt to relax and change his behavior. As Matt was able to relax more and understand Ann's insecurity, he was in a better frame of mind to calm her down, and even do something to boost her confidence. So, when Ann seemed insecure, Matt bought her flowers. When Ann felt clingy, she was required to go out, and workout for an hour. Within two weeks, both changed, and the relationship became stronger.

Here is an exercise. Write down a time when you were insecure or upset with your man. What is he doing specifically, to make you feel this way? What is your reaction? Now, sit for a few minutes with this, and analyze if this is an appropriate reaction to what you observe with your man. What is he doing specifically? Could it mean something else? Allow whatever upsets you to be released. Know that there are other explanations; so release the upsetting thoughts, so you come back to balance. Although this exercise can be intimidating, the end result will be freedom and release.

Love & Obey Rules #4: Live in Harmony

In order to create a strong successful relationship, you need to cultivate harmony in daily life. Today, there is so much infringement into our lives - work, duties, responsibilities, technology, social media and so much more. As the leaders, we must insist on harmony and balance. If everyone gets stressed out, it will be up to us to restore order, and not allow imbalances to continue for too long. The first thing I teach both men and women is to address any disagreements and disharmony, head on. Discuss and get past it. Don't let something remain unsaid, hoping it goes away. In my own relationship, I tend to end the day with a quick exchange of kisses and discussion. It brought me closer with my man, and I always reminded him that we don't go to bed angry or upset. It was difficult at first, because it felt like a chore, but it went a long way to maintaining harmony.

Our lives have changed so much; what used to be abnormal is now perfectly normal. Divorce has become normal with the rate at almost 50%, or all marriages may end in divorce. So, more than ever, we need real habits in place, to try to keep the relationship strong. What has not changed is a man's desire to protect and provide for his family.

If you want your Female Led Relationship to pan out, and thrive as a loving relationship with you as the leader, it is important to learn to never suppress his instincts. Let him have outlets for expressing them. Let him take care of you and provide for you, whether it's by paying the bills or building some shelves. Many men are drawn to construction projects, because they wish to explore their creativity. It's a stress relief from the drudgery of daily life. You have to take time for yourself, and give him time to explore these interests. When your man has submitted himself to your leadership, there is great trust. Never take it for granted or underestimate your power over him. But respect the position as his Queen and leader.

Love & Obey Rules #5: The head and heart phenomenon

Earlier, we discussed about how we girls, use speech as a main form of communication, while our guys may not say much, but are good with reading the energy we exude. This principle is one major aspect that we tend to ignore in many of our relationships, with the male gender as a whole.

Women are naturally more emotionally invested in situations and scenarios than men are. A man uses his head, "is it logical?" "What are the benefits?" "Would this be profitable or useful?" Such are the questions men ask before making decisions. Women think with their hearts. While this is a trait that has led us to achieve high goals and surmount great obstacles, it has also dumped us in a lot of trouble.

It can be glaringly clear to everyone around that this girl is being maltreated by her boyfriend or that he is using her, but she loves him very much, so all that occurs to her is how to make herself better for him, instead of just training him to love, respect and obey her.

During your training process with your man, work with logical, reasonable and direct words, so he can understand and assimilate what you are teaching him. Don't involve emotions or gut feelings during the training, or things will definitely get messy and spiral out of control.

The easiest trick to achieving success when training a man, especially one that isn't yet sure of his natural desire to submit to your authority or one that is unaware that he is being trained, is to let him see the logical reason why he should listen to you. If what you desire does not appeal to the sensible thinking process he has going on, you would be ignored and your training will backfire.

Love & Obey Rules #6: Understand Your Man's Natural Relationship Position.

There are two worlds- the outside world and your relationship world with your man. In the outside world, your man can be the originators of ideas, the one who leads everyone at the office, rescues people from the storm, the bread winner, and all that. In the world of your relationship, you're the boss. No matter how powerful and successful a man is in this outer world, he subconsciously and naturally desires to submit to your loving female authority, as his Queen Mother. Never try to change his leadership role in the world or his submissive role in your relationship. Even the CEOs of the Fortune 500 companies say, "Let me check with the misses about this weekend and see if it's okay." Harness the difference of these two worlds, and make it work in your favor from both sides.

I had a friend, who had a relationship with an outwardly domineering man. He had the kind of presence that just called people to follow him, and he just exuded competence. It took me a while to discover that she was in a Female Led Relationship with him. When I found out, I started observing them, and asking her questions. She explained to me that in the beginning, she would just give suggestions, and let him feel like he came up with an idea, until she gradually trained him to the point where she could correct him openly, without him feeling offended or feeling hurt. "He needs me to guide him," she told me one day. "He knows he is lost without me." Even when he leads in sexual activities, I guide him; I trained him to pay attention to my cues, in and out of the bedroom. Whether it's a soft moan that encourages him to continue what he is doing or an outright command to stop. You must always be working with his basic instincts; you should never forget this. Teach him how to take care of you in the language he understands. Anything else will most likely, break him or drive him away from you, and this is exactly the opposite of your aim. In this loving Female Led Relationship that you're making, sometimes, the key to leading it is to appear to follow in the beginning. In time, you both will know who rules the roost.

CHAPTER FIVE

--·--◇≈◇--·--

Female Relationship Leader is The Natural Evolution

Leadership is hard to define, and good leadership even harder, but if you can get people to follow you to the ends of the earth, you are a great leader.

–Indra Nooyi

S ince the beginning of time, women have always run the show in the relationship. So, a Female Led Relationship is a logical evolution. Let's look to the bible, to the very first relationship between the first man and woman - Adam and Eve. In the story, the serpent gives the apple to the woman because it knew that the woman was the more influential of the two. And Eve was successful in convincing Adam to taste the fruit, despite the fact that God gave him explicit instructions to not eat the fruit. Adam still succumbed to his wife, Eve's suggestion. There has long been a stigma with married men that they are "pussy whipped" or "hen pecked," meaning they are controlled by their women. But, the fact is that women have more power in the world and at home, than they realize.

Thanks to feminism, the modern woman has risen up, holding very high executive positions, being leaders, running fortune 500 companies, earning millions, running countries, all the while, being mothers and wives and running households. The idea of the "supermom" has been coined to be the woman who, like a superhero, is capable of doing it all. In the fascinating way evolution works, once the women of the world made up their minds to be better, they began to out-shine the men in several fields. The **Flynn effect** is the substantial and long-sustained increase in IQ test scores measured in many parts of the world, from roughly 1930 to the present day. However, when new test subjects take older IQ tests, in almost every case, their average scores are significantly higher than they were in that original time period. An IQ expert, James Flynn, believes the increasing rate of technology has stimulated our brains to work better. "The complexity of the modern world is making our brains adapt, and raising our IQ, but the facts are that women's IQ's have risen faster. According to Flynn, women have surpassed men on IQ tests in several countries including the US, Canada, New Zealand, and throughout Europe. In the US, about 60% of college graduates are women, and they are less likely to drop out than their male counterparts. In the 1980s, a woman, Marilyn Vos Savant, had the amazingly high IQ score of 228, according to the Guinness book of World Records.

More often than not, historically, we have seen men as smarter and physically stronger than women. But here are some studies that will make you reconsider those stereotypes you grew up to believe. Both science and math are considered subjects in which males are expected to perform better, due to the higher enrollment of boys to classes like engineering, chemistry, and quantum mechanics.

However, girls get overall higher grades in school, making them better than boys in science, even if they are not comfortable with the subject.

From kindergarten, girls show more self-regulation, than boys. They tend to follow rules, pay attention to specific instructions and details, as well as display an overall sense of self- pleasure by working through long term assignments, despite boredom and frustration. Girls are also, more likely to choose their homework before indulging in relaxing activities, like watching TV, reading or surfing the internet. Women are not equal to men; they are superior in many ways, and in most ways that will count in the future. It is not just a matter of culture or upbringing. It is a matter of chromosomes, genes, hormones, and nerve circuits. It is not mainly because of how experience shapes women, but because of intrinsic differences in the body and the brain. In the 1960s, professional schools had a handful of women in a class of a hundred. Today, they are approaching half of all the students at medical and law schools. More than 40 percent of students entering M.B.A. programs—the pool of future CEOs—are women. Yes, there are glass ceilings, but they are slowly being broken. Women make up 33 percent of federal district-court judges, almost 35 percent of federal appeals-court judges, and one- third of the U.S. Supreme Court. I've been noticing news items lately, about how women are gaining in many ways. They now represent a majority of U.S. college students, and 60% of all graduate students. Their income levels are rising, although they still don't have parity with men. They are far less involved in violent crimes, and crimes of all sorts. They are safer drivers. A child in a single-parent home is likely to be better off, if the parent is a woman. In the U.S., the odds are that 80% of the single parents will be women; having given birth, they stick around to raise children, while men are more likely to be missing. This role of raising our children has led young boys to look to the Mother more than the Father in modern society, and it is leading the way to the social change we are experiencing in the world. This dominance, at home and in the classroom by females, is starting to translate into dominance in the workforce, in business and in politics.

As women start to excel and become dominant in the workplace and in the business world, this is causing women to exert even more dominance within their personal relationships with men. Whereas, wives have always dominated their men behind closed doors in a subtle manner, now they are dominating their men more openly. They are taking charge of the bedroom, as they are becoming the initiators of sex. In Female Led Relationships, the emphasis is always on the women's pleasure, and the man is always trained to focus on her needs. Interestingly, the sex life in a Female Led Relationship is always highly rated by couples, and considered more intense and fulfilling for both partners. When a man focuses on the woman's pleasure, she is completely satisfied and in turn, allows the man to have his pleasure. This is so much different from relationships where men care only about their own pleasure, and the woman's pleasure is secondary.

You've heard of women faking orgasms, just to get through sex; this is one of the most destructive practices as at some point, enough resentment builds up, leaving both women and men feeling unsatisfied. As women exert more dominance in all areas of life, men's submissive natures are stirring, and men are desiring to be dominated in all areas of their lives by the female gender. Modern man is more eager than ever, to submit to a loving female Authority.

Some women are still restrained by traditions and societal expectations. Women naturally dominate men within the relationship, but not many women like to acknowledge that fact for fear of being societal outcasts. Some women still allow their men to appear as the "in-charge" and dominant partner, in order to conform to the model of what they witnessed from their parents. The female dominant nature still lies dormant in many women, and it often takes a male's submissive nature to draw it out. But as women become more successful and more aggressive in the classroom and in the business world, women are more readily embracing their dominant persona, and will gladly accept and even demand their male partner's submission. In my opinion, the couples that practice Female Led Relationships today, are in front of the societal curve. Female Led Relationships and male submission will be the foremost and normal sexuality of the future. I believe that a majority of women, who still consider it kinky and unusual today, will embrace this relationship in the not too distant future. Furthermore, their daughters will see the Mothers leading the household, and they will be stretching the acceptable limits and boundaries of Female Led Relationships in areas that we cannot imagine today.

According to researcher Israel Abramov of University of New York, women have a much more finely tuned ability to see slight variations in color than men do—which is why no straight man knows what "mauve" or "taupe" are, but all women do. Women also have a superior sense of hearing, and can distinguish between different scents, far better than men can. These very specific, detailed, finely tuned senses, along with "women's intuition", I believe this makes women better able to sense changes and adapt faster.

I am impressed with how confident and aggressive the younger women are today, compared to even 20 years ago. Women are running their own companies, moving up the corporate ladder faster, and breaking into positions, like President or Prime Minister, more than was ever done in history. The emergence of females in sports, where women were not allowed to compete, is another great indication of the power of women, and how it's increasing. Ivanka Trump believes a great part of her father's success on the ability to appeal to career minded modern woman. A hundred years ago, things were much different, where women were not even allowed to vote. It is this ability to evolve fast. I believe that gives women a tremendous advantage to take the lead in their relationships. There are so many examples of women in the highest positions of office today, when not too long ago, they were not even able to vote. The close race between President Trump and Hilary Clinton showed that North America is ready to be led by a woman. Many other countries are run by women, including, Germany, Denmark and Norway. Many women run large silicon valley companies, and have spearhead industries into new frontiers with their genius. I suspect that in the future, women will be running the world. The societal evolution that is taking place cannot be stopped. Men are sensing this change, and many are happy to step into the submissive role. The International Journal of Business Governance and Ethics, published a research concluding that female led companies are more successful than the ones led by males. A Pew Research poll found that the public agrees— women make fairer, more compassionate, and more trustworthy leaders than men do. Over the 20 years surveyed, women in Congress introduce more bills, attract more co-sponsors and bring home, more money for their districts than their male counterparts on average. Women are intuitive, and better able to understand emotions and body language, making them rational thinkers and team coordinators.

Of course the desire for Female Led Relationships is nothing new. The book, "Venus in Furs" by Leopold Von Sacher-Masoch, was written over 130 years ago. It is about a man with strong submissive fantasies. He worships the Goddess Venus, and he pursues his fantasies when he meets a wealthy woman named Wanda, with whom he starts a romance. Some have credited "Venus in Furs" with propelling Female Led Relationships into the mainstream of the society, more than 130 years ago. So, we are on the cusp of this relationship trend, but it is not a new idea. But, I believe with the evolution of women and their current roles in the society, the Female Led Relationship is ripe to explode into the society.

Female Led Relationships Is not BDSM

It is important to emphasize that Female Led Relationships is not BDSM. Hollywood and news media sensationalism, enjoy grouping dominant strong women into the BDSM world. Where one is entertainment focused solely on a man's desire to be humiliated by his "dominatrix", this still places the male in the spotlight. Female led is a female power position in the relationship. It's about the female's needs first. It has nothing to do with whipping or humiliation. BDSM has very little to do with a healthy relationship between men and women. It's much more of a perversion, and it should be avoided if you want to create a successful Female Led Relationship. Female Led Relationship uses Mother energy. BDSM is demeaning, perverted and even though it appears the woman is in a power position in BDSM because she is the dominant, she is actually submitting to a male, who just wants his own desires for pain and perversion to be satisfied.

BDSM is not the subject of this book, but, it is important that both you and your man understand that, creating a loving open Female Led Relationship does not involve humiliation or suppression or tearing down of your man. As mentioned before, in BDSM, women are not acting from a place of power because they are acting out a man's fantasy. This is the opposite of true power, where your man is actually serving you and happy to do so. Now, there can be opportunities where a woman chooses to dominate her man sexually, and her man wants to be submissive, but this still begins with your desire in a loving exchange with your man.

Different Types of Female Led Relationships

All Female Led Relationships are not the same. Some are just restricted to what happens during love-making, others become an entire lifestyle. You are free to create any type of relationship you desire. If you prefer to keep it confined to the bedroom to spice up love-making, that's perfectly acceptable. But the real power and evolution of the relationship occurs when it becomes a lifestyle. Your man will enjoy serving your needs all day. He'll open doors for you, bring you your slippers, give you a mini neck massage, and wait for you to initiate love-making. He would make you your coffee, or serve you your breakfast. I had the experience in my own relationship, when I was once traveling on a business trip and returning, and my man showed up at the airport with flowers; he took me home and surprised me, having re-decorated our room into a queen's palace, complete with satin sheets and Egyptian cotton robe. This was just one example of how he wanted to incorporate treating me as a pampered Queen. Another example is when we go to fairs, or festivals, he returns with a secret gift, which he picked up for me. It's the focus; always on my needs, which defines this relationship. But, we both enjoyed the Female Led Relationship. It has created a whole new world of exploring in our relationship; keeping the spice alive and creating fun. Again, that's what's great about the Female Led Relationship- it can be incorporated just creating more intimate times, or little treats like a spontaneous foot or neck rub. The whole point is to create a relationship that both you and your man will enjoy.

Some of my friends have a set aside one night out, where they will go to a restaurant or take a weekend off, away from the kids, to be with their partner. I suggest even having an hour every 2 days, where it's parent's hour. There is less stress to take an entire day off, but allows you and your spouse or boyfriend to connect in a meaningful way, without interruption. In addition, encouraging little practices, like allowing my man to be the gentleman, opening doors and allowing me to enter first, made him feel more masculine. Though I was the leader in the relationship, he still felt empowered in his role as my man and protector.

The most important part of the successful Female Led Relationship, or any relationship, requires trust and honesty. When a man trusts his woman enough to open up to her about his deepest, most hidden natural desires, this sets the stage for intimacy on a more meaningful level. The sad fact is that, many men must keep their innermost desires, hidden. But for those couples who dare to be uninhibited about their desires, they open themselves up to a special kind of intimacy. The man who trusts his woman enough to submit his entire being to her will, bonds with his woman on a level that few men have experienced. Likewise, when the woman is trustworthy enough to rule her man with love, this causes them to bond together in a way that most traditional relationships cannot enjoy. To these couples, this relationship is more than sexual. It is spiritual.

Female Led in Media

I believe that the society is evolving into a female led society. Women are beginning to take charge on a social and globally emotional level. Hollywood and Madison Avenue are capitalizing on the ever-growing male submissive nature, as movies, television, and advertising are celebrating the powerful woman. Although the real strength of a woman is in her intellectual, social and sexual power, it is easier to show female power via physical strength. Thus, movies like Wonder Woman, Resident Evil and

Atomic Blonde, and TV shows such as "Super Girl", "Dark Angel" and "Alias" are popular and thriving. Men are yielding to the intellectual, social and sexual power in women, and this causes them to desire to be conquered in the physical by the Female as well. This is where a lot of the female wresting fantasies that men have originate from. It is also why Hollywood and television have capitalized on this "desire to experience the powerful female" theme in so many productions. Many of the directors for these movies are men and so, they find it difficult to showcase what it is that is the inner power of a woman; so they express it by showing the women as having physical or super power. When a woman kicks a man around on television or in the movies, chances are the male viewers are sexually turned on. This is because this act represents the power of the female, and men want to submit to it. Just look at some popular movies that made it big in the box office; "Cat Woman" "Snow White and the Huntsmen", "Charlie's Angels", Terminator 3", "The Matrix Reloaded", "Dare devil" and "Lara Croft, Tomb Raider." All of these films have strong, leather wearing female characters, with scenes where they physically beat up men. Men know that the real power of women is sexual and intellectual, but movies and television simplify it into the physical displays of violence.

The one movie that I believe is a masterpiece and truly captures the sexual power of a woman is "Basic Instinct." The Sharon Stone character, Catherine Tramell, dominated the so-called intelligent men in the movie by using her sexual power, combined with her sharp intellect. The director, Paul Verhoeven, was successful in showing the sexual power of women over men, through her character. Remove the psychotic and Hitchcock-like thriller aspects, and "Basic Instinct" is a movie about a dominant woman, who has her way with the weaker male gender.

Unfortunately, Hollywood rarely takes the time to develop this aspect of a woman's nature and will instead, revert to only the physical when they want to show a powerful woman. A number of men went to see the leather wearing, whip wielding Halle Berry as Cat Woman. Too bad, the producers and writers did not recognize the full potential of the movie and consequently, did not truly develop *Cat Woman's* sexual power.

The *Cat Woman* character in the 1960's, "Batman" television program played an important role in taking Female Led Relationships into the mainstream. *"Cat Woman"* was a major influence in igniting the submissive nature within boys, as well as, within grown men. When I counsel or interview men, it never ceases to amaze me how many of them will point to two female television characters from the 1960's, when describing their earliest recollection of having submissive desires. They point to Julie Newman as *Cat Woman,* and Diana Rigg as the leather wearing Emma Peel of "The Avengers." Both of these women were dominant, they wore dominating leather clothing, and they radiated with a dominant female sexuality. *"Cat Woman"* left a lasting impression on the sexuality of many men, as they would watch Batman or better yet, boyish Robin, being tied up and teased by the leather clad and sexy female. The psychological and sociological symbolism of such a scene was very profound, as it portrayed how a powerful woman renders men weak and helpless. It was a fantasy that males could identify with because such scenes stirred their naturally submissive nature.

The male desire for Female Led Relationships is evident throughout Pop Culture, and the smart female knows how to capitalize. Taylor Swift, Queen B and Madonna, have been able to combine music, sexuality and female power into Pop Culture empires. Their popularity and fan following rivals that of the Beatles and Elvis. Madonna's music and music videos portray an aggressive, sexual and strong woman. Much like Pop Culture itself, Madonna has evolved from being suggestive about female Dominance (Blonde Ambition) to openly portraying female domination in her music and videos (Erotica).

Shania Twain is another Pop Culture Diva, who has successfully combined her music with a public image that depicts female dominance and power. Although her music is of the traditionally more conservative country variety, Shania is not unaccustomed to posing in provocative female domination style clothing in her videos or while on stage (including in front of a worldwide audience during the Super Bowl), and many of her songs celebrate the strong woman. The music of Shania appeals to a totally different audience than that of Madonna, but both of these women have ascended to the top of their extremely competitive industry by appealing to man's desire for female dominance. While both women are very talented from an artistic standpoint, what has brought them success beyond imagination is the dominant and sexual aura they portray. The sexual, powerful female captivates men, and Pop Culture in the new Millennium is not shy about promoting the dominant female, or capitalizing on the submissive nature of man.

Here in the new Millennium, the battle of the sexes is over, but women never viewed it as a battle. Women are no longer deceived into being submissive.

They are assuming their true natures. Men are moving into secondary as they watch their women take over. Nevertheless, it still often takes a submissive man to support the dominant woman. We need it. I have had witnesses that accept their inner fantasies of their women in-charge; it changes the dynamic of the relationship fast. Women are accustomed to taking charge now, in their careers, and in the household. They can instinctively, naturally take over in the bedroom. I think when we sense the submissive energy of our men, we react subconsciously to it.

The male Love & Obey zone is a tranquil, and somewhat a hypnotic state that comes from the absolute surrender of the human's will. The male Love & Obey zone is obtained within males, when they surrender their will and their power over to a female. When a woman dominates a man mentally and emotionally, there is an energy and a power that she releases. This energy demands and desires submission from the man. When a man surrenders to this power coming from the female, he enters into the Love & Obey zone. As he lets go and yields himself to the woman, he disarms his conscience guard, and he allows his submissive nature to be released. This causes him to enter into that tranquil and near hypnotic state. Once a man enters the Love & Obey zone, he typically never wants to leave it. In addition, the sex he experiences in it is almost always described as the best he ever had.

The male Love & Obey zone is a place of absolute surrender, where the female rules supreme. It is a magical place within the psyche of a man, where he worships a woman with his spirit. It is powerful and it is beautiful. Only a man who surrenders his will to a woman and enters the Love & Obey zone, can fully see a woman in all her beauty and glory.

One woman told me, "After I've pleasured my man, or allowed him to pleasure me, he kind of lays there, he tilts his head to the side, he gets a grin on his face, and his eyes kind of get glazed over." Her man had entered the Love & Obey zone. That look she was referring to is the look of tranquility, contentment, submission, and genuine love. That look is what the Female Led Relationship lifestyle is all about. By dominating and disciplining her man, she struck a chord within him. The Love & Obey male desires to be dominated and pleasured by a woman. Most men long for this inside, and spend a good portion of their lives searching for this void to be filled within them. Once they experience the strong yet, loving hand of a dominant female whom they trust and love, it fulfills them and it brings to them, tranquility and contentment. Her man had achieved a deep Love & Obey zone experience.

If all women could see that look on their man's face or feel that kind of intimacy, they would flock to this lifestyle. Unfortunately, many women just see Hollywood and the media's leather outfits, the whips, and the techniques that dominant women in music videos and movies used to get their men into that magical state of deep submission, and they think that this lifestyle is "strange" or "bizarre."

If they would only look past the superficial Hollywood portrayal of dominant women, and see the intellectual and emotional techniques that female Leaders utilize, and if they would instead, focus on the results that they bring, if only they would realize that there are different aspects and methods for participating in this female led way of life, then I believe that most women would openly embrace the Female Led Relationship lifestyle. We want to connect with our man in a way that goes all the way to our souls. We females in general, desire this level of "spiritual" intimacy with our men. If they would only understand that most men need to be dominated, pleasured, and controlled by a woman in order to have peace within themselves, then I am convinced the majority of women would assume their proper place, which is to be the female Leader.

Female Led Relationships are still a minority lifestyle between couples. Hollywood films about it, music videos and pornography on the internet all thrive in our society because the majority of submissive men still must seek out female Led experiences outside of his home. Many men are eager to surrender themselves over to their wives, but they hesitate because they fear their wives might think this desire they have is bizarre, not manly, and refuse to participate with them. The biggest obstacle to a Female Led Relationship is still the reluctance of the female to take charge. This just goes to show how successful our male dominated patriarchal society has been in making women feel inferior to men. As women, we have been programmed, since childhood, that the man should be the dominant partner in a relationship and society. It is never easy to overcome a thousand years of our traditions. Women still struggle with the thought that a Female Led Relationship is "weird or abnormal."

The first time I was exposed to this lifestyle, I thought it to be strange and even perverted. I went into it, viewing these people as being sexually dysfunctional. However, I soon learned that most of these people were healthy and normal. They were people from all walks of life, religious backgrounds, and professions, that were members of the Female Led parties and groups I attended. Now, I will confess that there are extremes that people go to with BDSM that are not healthy, but that is the same with all things. Eating is not a negative habit, but when taken to extremes, it can be unhealthy. The same goes for a person's sexuality. From my years of studying and living this Female Led Relationship lifestyle, I can tell you that the desire of a man to submit to a woman is not perverted. It is natural. As a matter of fact, it is very common among men. I believe it is the number one sexual desire among men living in our society today. Perversion is defined as that which is outside the sexual normal. Female domination and male submission are very much within the norm of people's intellectual, emotional and sexual desires.

What women must keep in mind about Female Led Relationships is the fact that, men need it as much as they do, maybe, more. It is almost always the man who will introduce the Female Led Relationship lifestyle to the woman. A courageous man, with submissive desires, is usually the catalyst to introduce a Female Led Relationships to his Female partner. Why do men do this? It's because men desire and need to be in submission to women. No matter how hard the society or religion tries to tell men differently, a deep natural desire and basic instinct inside of them yearns to surrender to a powerful woman. These desires grow stronger with age, and men will spend countless hours, dreaming and fantasizing about Female Led Relationships. Men will pursue these desires, and struggle with these desires, trying to come to terms with them but sadly, a man will not come to terms with these desires until he truly has a relationship with a woman that can explore these desires with him in a loving manner.

The other side of this dynamic is that, women, who embrace the dominant role and who allow their dominant nature to come out, end up absolutely loving this lifestyle. It never ceases to amaze me how many women, who once were really hesitant about being dominant, end up loving it so much that they later say that they would never go back to being in submission to a man, or only having vanilla "male led" sex with a man. This lifestyle is liberating to women, and it is also liberating for men, as they can now fulfill that natural yearning within them.

The number of couples who practice the Female Led Relationships lifestyle, has exploded over the past twenty years. Most of these couples keep it private, but I can testify from the number of letters I receive, that Female Led Relationships are on the rise in our society. It may not enjoy a plurality yet, but one only needs to look at the trends and the societal evolution that is taking place to see what is transpiring. As women continue to become dominant in college, in business and in politics as the leaders of nations, more women will naturally take the dominant role in their relationships. This is great news for the submissive male and Females around the world.

As far as the Hollywood BDSM fantasies go, it depends on each woman and on each relationship. A Female Led Relationships can take on, many forms. Lots of dominant women do enjoy the whole leather and Hollywood BDSM style, and flare in their lifestyle, and do use these tools in the training and "the disciplining" of their men, as well as, adding fun and excitement to their sex lives. Other women enjoy a softer Female Led Relationship, as they prefer an intellectual and emotional type of pleasure and training, of their men. Still, other women love to be the dominant partner and love to rule the relationship, but they do not like to incorporate much sex into it. Some women are Queen Mothers, while other women see themselves as feminists, and others see themselves as equals with men, while still holding on to the secret belief that the woman needs to lead the man. As I mentioned, I am opposed to the dark side of BDSM. I do not believe that men should be humiliated, feminized, or treated with cruelty of any sort, physically or emotionally. However, some playfulness with costumes, and this sort of fun side of the Hollywood and music video portrayal and costumes, can be spicy at times.

The most important thing is that, each couple must keep the lines of communication open, as honesty and openness are crucial in any relationship. A woman has to be open minded to explore new things, as her partner shares with her, his deepest desires to submit. It is all about negotiation and fulfillment. I ask women, what touches his submissive nature? Does he view you as his Queen? If so, then behave like a Queen. Does he view you as his super hero chick? Does he crave a Goddess to worship? Does he enjoy the helpless feeling of being under your control? I tell women to find out what stirs her man's submission and then, do these things to him. A smart woman will take a man's submission, and channel it into his service of her. A shrewd woman will have a life of unending pleasure, if she channels her man's submissive tendencies intelligently. A wise woman will use her dominance to draw out more of her man's submission and then, use that submission to get her needs met and fulfilled in every way.

I like to equate the Female Led Relationship to a dance. The man seduces the female's dominant nature with his submissive nature. She then, begins to draw out more of his submissive nature with her dominant nature, which draws out even more of her dominance, which draws out more of his submission, and so on. This dynamic works much like a magnetic force, with two opposites attracting. The Female's dominance feeds off of the man's submission, and his submission feeds off of her dominance. One needs the other to thrive and to grow. It is similar to how the plant world and the animal world function, with the plants giving us the oxygen we need and we in return, give the plants the carbon dioxide they need. As we breathe in their gift, we give them our gift, as we exhale. So, it is with dominance and submission. The Female Leader gives the male what he needs by dominating him, and the male gives her his gift by submitting to her, and treating her like his Queen.

Most women want to have a man that loves, honors, worships, and obeys her. Young girls dream about Prince Charming, who comes along and treats her like a Queen. What woman wouldn't want a man to focus all his energy and his attention on her all of the time? A man that would pamper her, give her foot and body massages, and who would get more pleasure out of pleasuring her, than receiving pleasure himself. How about a man that would do whatever you tell him to do, without arguing or complaining? A man that would not only do all of his chores, like cutting the grass and washing the cars, but would also do some housework, the laundry, the grocery shopping, or even the cooking. How about a man that would wine and dine her, and shower her with gifts? What woman would not want a man that would love her with all of his heart, and who would view her as his earthly Goddess? When we read novels, we desire to have the men we see in those books; loving, attentive, caring and absolutely miserable, when we aren't happy. The dominant female lives this dream because she has learned how to motivate her man to serve her needs, by meeting his need to be dominated.

This lifestyle is a large umbrella that encompasses a wide variety of lifestyles and activities. The common denominator is that, the woman is the dominant partner. A Female Led Relationship is important because, while it is a desire that primarily expresses itself in a woman's sexuality, it reflects the core desire within the male gender. It is that male's desire for loving female authority that ultimately empowers women, one relationship at a time.

The Making of a Relationship Leader

I like to define a relationship leader as a loving authority; someone who is in charge of the entire activities and people in a specific place; in this case, the relationship. The leader does not need to be feared or despised; in fact, that makes the people following you unwilling to obey. And as we have emphasized, the relationship is between two consenting adults. The journey to becoming the best relationship leader you can possibly become is different for everyone. It might take many years for some, or be just a breeze for others. The key to beginning this journey, however, is to realize the need for you to be a relationship leader, and your man to be your obedient and loving gentleman. You can know this once you fully realize who your man is, and what he needs from you. The Natural Man Laws and the Love & Obey Rules are what will guide you on your journey. Here are a couple of techniques that will help transform you into the relationship leader you need to become:

The Female Leadership Craft #1:

Project Calm, Assertive Energy.

You're seeing this and thinking, "Oh, this again!" Yes, we have mentioned it several times, but this is because it cannot be overemphasized. The natural submissive state in a man comes out when there is a calm assertive female around. When you project confident positive energy, he is willing to obey, because you seem sure of what you are asking him to do.

In a relationship where the man is submissive and the woman is not dominant, the man will try to fill the void by trying to become the relationship leader. This of cause, is a recipe for disaster. He does not know the first thing about being a good leader; so he is nervous. He will then, try to mask this nervousness by becoming aggressive and lashing out. This is how many females begin to experience domestic violence in their homes. When loving and nurturing women lead and obedient gentlemen follow, there are no domestic violence issues.

THE CRAFT IN ACTION

How to Change Your Energy

As I've said, your energy will determine how your man sees you in your role as a Relationship Leader. All your energy—good and bad—is a reflection of your state of body, mind, and intention. Calm, assertive energy, for instance, reveals itself with a confident demeanor, straight shoulders, a deliberate gait, and the clear-sightedness that comes from knowing exactly what you want from this moment. If you want to be a Queen, you must present yourself with the regal poise of a Queen. The following exercises will help you identify your current energy and the energy of those around you, by focusing on two opposing states: positive and negative.

Identifying Positive Energy

It helps to have a partner or a mirror for this exercise:

1. Standing in front of a trusted friend (or mirror), think about a time when you have felt truly positive about life. Picture yourself at a happy, expansive moment, and channel that energy. Close your eyes if it helps. For a minute or two, do your best to put yourself back in that positive state of mind.

2. Adjust your body to match your "positive state of mind." Notice what's happening to your arms, chest, shoulders, and facial expression. How are you breathing?

3. If you're with someone, ask that person to mirror any changes he or she notices. Like I've said, energy is

contagious, and influences those around you. Ask that person to demonstrate to you, the way your body changed as you filled yourself with positive thoughts.

4. Being aware of your energy is the first step toward changing it. In the hours or days after this exercise, try to replicate the positive energy state you created. Even if you are not feeling good, adjusting your body and mind in a positive direction can have a powerful impact on the energy you convey to the world, and to your man. Think about a Queen; even when the kingdom is in turmoil, a great Queen will project confidence, and lead her royal subject with a calm authority.

Identifying Negative Energy

Do this exercise with a partner, or in front of a mirror:

1. Picture yourself at a time when you were feeling down, angry, or frustrated. For a minute or two, put yourself in that negative state of mind.

2. Adjust your body to match the negative state of mind. Notice what's happening to your arms, chest, shoulders, and facial expression. How has your breathing changed?

3. If you're with someone, ask that person to mirror any changes he or she notices in your body language. Negative energy is just as contagious as positive energy, and influences those around you. Ask that person to show you the way your body and energy changed, as you filled your head with negative thoughts and fear or anxiety.

4. Take a deep breath, and return to the positive state from the first part of the exercise. For a minute or two, bring your mind back to that happy, powerful, inspired state. Notice how much control you have over your positive and negative states of mind.

5. You may try repeating these exercises with your man near you, to see what kind of reaction occurs with your man. How does he act when your energy changes? You can also practice with your children. Once you understand how you are directly affecting others, you will become more conscious of your own energy, and how it can influence your man.

The Female Leadership Craft #2:

Find your balance of discipline, "love and affection"

The ability to strike a balance between these two aspects of your relationship is very important if your goal is having a relationship with a properly trained, well balanced gentleman. Some of you will cringe at the sight of the word, discipline. This is because in your minds, you have associated the word with punishment or cruelty. Disciplining a person can be achieved with love and affection, even if the discipline sounds stern or strict on the surface. Look at a well- trained army unit for example, when you see them, they project unity, they work like a well-oiled machine. They all know the rules, and behave accordingly. You don't think they are "being treated cruelly;" you think they are disciplined. The Leader of an army unit may be tough and strict, but he is doing it to protect and save the lives of his men on the battle field. He is acting from a place of love and affection. This is because they have been trained to follow a fundamental set of rules. Such is the goal of having discipline in your relationship. When you go out and he opens doors for you, pulls out your chair and behaves like an all-round gentleman, you nod in appreciation to him and at home, you read each other's cues; you become a well-oiled relationship machine. He knows the rules, and he obeys them. Everybody that sees you together begins to admire your special connection.

The Female Leadership Craft #3:

Establish Your Rules and Always Enforce Them.

Every organized social unit, whether it's military or not, needs proper, clear-cut rules. Of course, where there are rules, there must be an enforcer; someone who makes sure the rules are followed. In the Female Led Relationship this has to be you. You will need to be a leader, not a dictator. Allow him to make contributions to your relationship rules. This will help him to be more willing to follow them. Now, remember, the first quality of an enforcer is that you must also follow the rules. If you are breaking the rules and expecting him to follow them, he will not take Female Led Relationship training seriously. You will need to reward his obedience. When he does even little tasks, like running you a bath, massaging your feet, cooking, or buying you feminine products, offer him something in return - he can go out and hang-out with his friends, or let him go to his favorite basketball of NFL game, or surprise him with tickets to his favorite concert. You want to motivate him to do more and more everyday, to please you. If your man initiates sex, as men will often do, you must do your best to respond positively. Men are very sensitive to women and their willingness to engage in sex. In some cases, it will be up to you to initiate as well. But use it as a moment to have your partner relax and pamper you.

The Female Leadership Craft #4:

Be a Good Leader and Give Him Attention

I remember at the end of one of my longer relationships, my partner indicated that I was not present in the relationship. He felt that I left him alone. I learned, even back then, the importance of not giving the impression that you are not interested. Men need constant attention. Couples that play together, stay together. Go out, work out, go camping on weekends, cook, laugh, and sleep together. These may seem unimportant, but the time you spend together makes all the difference. You want to grow and evolve together? Make every experience an opportunity to learn about your man. I often ask mini questions of women in long term relationships about their men. I was always surprised to see how many women were unaware of basic facts about their men. What's his favorite place to visit ? What would he rather be doing if he did not have to work ? What's the one sexual act he's always wanted to try? Often, women know a lot of facts like his shirt size, shoe size, his favorite foods. But often, they had no idea about inner hidden desires, or fantasies. Ladies, it is your responsibility to know and fulfill your man's fantasies. So you need to shower him with attention, and continue to know everything about him. He's your life partner. A good Queen must always know his faithful subject. When you know what makes him tick, you can begin to work on him, reward him, so he never has to go elsewhere to be fulfilled.

Put your attention on him, but do not smother him. On the flip side, don't be jealous or too clingy. Don't be confrontational, like questioning his whereabouts or what he did that day. Attention will be welcomed, but clingy criticism will only upset him.

The Female Leadership Craft #5: Read Your Man's Body Language.

Previously, we learned that we need to be mindful of our energy; now, we need to be mindful of our man's body language, as well as, energy. Be aware of it, as it will tell you a lot about what he is feeling inside. The first thing to note is that, a man behaves completely different from a woman. A man will not tell you things he is feeling inside. You have to read it from his behavior. Be sensitive if his energy is low. You do not want him to be over worked or exhausted. They are not great at handling stress like we are, and he is not able to approach the relationship with enthusiasm if his energy is low. At times like these, he needs a break. Adjust his nutrition. Make him smoothies, with fresh fruit and vegetables, or encourage him to increase his hydration. You have the responsibility of deciding what the family is consuming. So, if your man seems excessively tired or weak, then he may need a break or a reboot. The second thing to note is your man's disposition. Is he generally happy with life, or is he depressed? Does he seem distant or withdrawn. These are times which call for more communication or activities, in order to increase your personal time. Sometimes, when there is a new baby in the house, men can feel alienated and cast aside. You will have to take the lead at times like this, and if you notice these moods, it's important to address it.

CHAPTER SIX

--⸺⸺◆⸺⸺--

The Superior Sex

Why would physically stronger males, who live in a patriarchal world, have this desire to submit to the so- called weaker sex? Is it sexual? Are men so captivated by

the beauty of the female that they feel inferior? Sexuality does play a role. Men have feared the beauty and sexuality of women from the beginning of human history. That is why some religions have tried to cover up women, and force them into conservatism. They feel this makes them powerless, and prevents the man from becoming controlled. I think these civilizations knew that men cannot resist the beauty of the female and her power. Our modern fashion forward society, purposely dresses women for success, and puts them in a power position with the ability to dress, showing off as much as they want. This, in itself, shows how women have the power because even men are still restricted to suits or business casual. If a man wears a dress or skirt, it's frowned upon, whereas a woman has the freedom to wear suits, dresses, skirts, shorts, casual, dressy, elegant or dowdy. I believe that most women are unaware of how much power, even this kind of freedom can give. There are many other ways where women have been given freedom over men. If a woman accidentally enters a man's restroom, nothing will happen, but if a man accidentally went into the women's restroom, he is likely to be arrested. Women can quickly expose their breasts at a topless beach, but men can never expose the penis, unless it's a nudist beach, where both go naked. Women are allowed to have almost a year maternity leave in some countries, but men would have up to a few months, even if his role was to stay home and care for children. So, there are numerous instances where women are slowly gaining more and more advantages. But it hasn't always been this way; Christian denominations that require women to wear a covering for their heads and forbids them to wear make-up, or Muslim religions that require women to wear veils and dress in clothing that covers their entire bodies, enforce these rules because religion fears the sexuality of women and places burdens on women, because men cannot control their sexual thoughts and urges. Women are mysterious to men, and men marvel at the beauty of the female. Women give off a sexual energy that men cannot resist. However, these religions are of the belief that women should always be subservient to men. Even today, women can still experience being second. Wages are still a battle. In Hollywood, it is fact that men are paid more than women- sometimes millions. Sexual misconduct - until this year, many women remained silent about sexual harassment, especially in the workplace. There are stories where women were forced to remain silent, or paid to "go away" - Harvey Weinstein and Cosby are just two of the dozens of high profile cases, where women finally, were able to discuss the sexual harassment they experienced at the hands of powerful men. So, the advantages that women now enjoy came after years and years of battling and fighting, to increase equality. But, it's slowly changing. Men are feeling women's power, and in many ways, they welcome it. The millennial generation see no real difference between what women and men can achieve. However, women were never the weaker sex. There are many examples of where women have the power of a super human, with handling all their responsibilities and expected to look gorgeous, have perfect bodies, be the leader, gain respect, earn money, and do all of these with grace and charm. Even with all the changes, you will never see women hanging out having drinks after work, while the man runs home to take care of dinner and the kids. Only in movies, like "Bad Moms". It is interesting that moms, who go out partying and are assertive, are considered "Bad". However, women rise to the occasion everyday, regardless of the pressures. Today, women can do anything - athletes, CEO's, celebrities, trail blazers, astronauts or super moms. It's only oppressive laws and customs which kept women in a subservient position. But, women are indeed powerful and they are more encouraged to speak out, and be assertive with the focus on female heroine in movies, or females speaking out in media. The "Timesup" campaign are all real examples of movements showing the power of women to band together, and fight against the status quo. What is clear is that, men can only become the dominant sex by enforcing oppressive laws and customs against women. It is not natural for men to be the dominant sex. It is natural for men to serve women. In nature, the male's sole focus is on fighting for the female, and protecting and feeding her. The female's purpose is to ensure continuation of the species. So, it is only natural that with such an important task, women make the best leaders. If it's good enough for mother nature, it's good enough for human nature.

I think society tends to misjudge the softness and the gentleness of women for weakness and submission. But, it is this ability to be sensing and intuitive that help women to survive. Likewise, society has mistaken the toughness and the macho ways of men for strength. Men are only stronger physically, and even this is being challenged, as more women lift weights and do powerlifting. I did weight-lifting and powerlifting for years as exercise, until I was stronger than most men my height and weight. Women also possess the real strength, which is Intellectual, Emotional, Spiritual, and Sexual. Unfortunately, most women are unaware of their power because of a pervasive myth, that they are the inferior sex.

Religion is where men are responsible for spreading a lot of myths regarding women. Judaism, Christianity and Islam, were founded by patriarchal beliefs, and male supremacy was reflected in their theology. In many fundamentalist sects, wives are taught to be subservient to their men. To obey. Why? Catholics, Muslims and traditional Jews restrict their priesthoods to men. Why? Why must the god of all humans be approached only through men? Why is god in traditional, thought to be a man? Why not a Goddess, who rules the universe?

My feeling is that, a fundamental shift is taking place. Women were not viewed as well-adapted for leadership roles in primitive and early historical times. But our emerging world economy is becoming less based on physical strength, and more dependent on intelligence and emotional balance. Women are not wired to see disagreement as a challenge to themselves. Women value common welfare above singular success. Women are more open to cooperation than competition. Women have evolved to focus more on prudent long- term survival, and less on immediate gains. When women give birth and spend months suckling an infant, they understand better, that we all depend on each other. They're programmed to nurture the defenseless, plan for the future, value others for their qualities, rather than for their external traits. Here are some biological facts that are undeniable when one looks at the research. Women have better senses (smell, touch, taste, and sight).

After all, they have to endure the equivalent of a bowling ball popping out of their vagina every time they give birth. But an episode of the show, "MythBusters", proved that women can hold their hands in freezing water, 19% longer than those of crybaby men.

A study at Aston University in England concluded that, women are better than men at remembering things two minutes, 15 minutes, and 24 hours after learning them. A Mayo Clinic study said that, not only do women naturally have a better sense of memory than men, the gap widens with age. Researchers, at the University of Western Ontario, concluded that women are far better than men at handling the stress of job interviews. Female brains also secrete more oxytocin—AKA the "cuddle hormone"—than male brains, making women calmer under fire, than men are.

The University of Western Ontario found that women handle the stress of a job interview better than men. It was found that women come better prepared by researching the company, and having mock interviews with friends before the final day. Men, on the other hand, took things easy and only prepared at the last minute. So much for the inferior or weaker sex. But that is biological, what about intellectual? Women are readers and learners. We are very open to, and interested in finding ways to continuously improve our personal skills. This focus on our development makes us more self-aware, which enables us to have a very strong emotional intelligence; a key trait of successful leaders.

Women are natural cheerleaders. We love discovering what motivates people into action, and we are excited to hand out words of encouragement, thank you, gifts for jobs well done, and pats on the back, which could explain why Gallup's 2015 State of the American Manager report says that, people who work for women leaders are more engaged than those who work for men. Perhaps, the most influential person to come to the conclusion that women are the superior gender and better leaders than men, was Dr. Ashley Montagu. Dr. Montagu was the author of more than sixty books. Montagu wrote books on anthropology, human anatomy, intelligence, and relationship. His last book published was, "The Natural Superiority of Women", originally published in 1952, and updated four times. The fifth edition was published in 1999, and has been expanded and modernized to fortify Dr. Montagu's theme that women are superior to men.

The book argues that the female of the species is biologically, sexually, emotionally, and even intellectually superior to the male. Dr. Montagu writes that women possess humane intelligence that will enable women to steer society toward a more humanized condition. Dr. Montagu used his knowledge of physical anthropology to dispel the myth of conventional wisdom, that women are the "weaker sex", by showing how women's biological, genetic, and physical makeup makes her not only man's equal, but his superior. Dr. Montagu explains that his thesis is supported by scientific evidence. Here is some of his evidence from his book, "The Natural Superiority of Women"- "The evidence indicates that woman is, on the whole, biologically superior to man." "The evidence is clear: from the constitutional standpoint, woman is the stronger sex. The explanation of the greater constitutional strength of the female lies largely, if not entirely, in her possession of two complete X- chromosomes, and the male's possession of only one." "From infancy to adulthood, the female superiority in verbal or linguistic functions, is consistent and marked." "Girls excel in most tests of memory. They do significantly better on tests of picture memories, and such tests as copying a bead chain from memory." "As far as intelligence scores and other indicators of what we call intelligence, the conclusion is clear: Girls do better than boys. In short, the age-old myth that women are of inferior intelligence to men has, as far as the scientific evidence goes, not a leg to stand upon."

"Women continue to grow in intelligence; and in the kind of intelligence that is of great importance, for the survival of the human race. I think it can be shown that women far outdistance men." "Studies carried out at both Duke University and at the University of London, uniformly agree that woman are far better judges of character than men, yet another evidence of woman's higher problem solving abilities." "With respect to psychological and social qualities, the facts again, it seems to me, prove that women are superior to men." "Women are the bearers, the nurturers of life; men have more often, tended to be the curtailers, the destroyers of life." A woman, who doesn't know what she is entitled to, will never reach out to claim what is rightfully hers. Women are born, designed by biology, society, and the environment to be the leaders where they find themselves. Don't let this great gift go to waste. Harness it, use it for the benefit of those you love, and you will be shocked at the great improvements you will begin to notice in your homes and relationships.

During my time of attending Female Led parties and meetings, I met many men who harbored a deep desire to be in a Female Led Relationship, and be sexually dominated by a woman. I had heard, from dozens of men, about their submissive fantasies, starting when they were teenagers. Often, they don't know where it originates from, but they recall a scene in a movie or television program, where a woman was aggressive or dominant with a man, and how they became extremely sexually aroused. The common thread is that, when a woman is portraying any kind of dominant image in a movie, magazine or a book, they become weak. Even just a certain look on a woman's face in an advertisement, can cause a man to be overcome with submissive feelings toward the female gender.

They tell me how images or stories of women being the sexual aggressor excite them, whether it's an older woman who seduces and sexually dominates younger men or any other scene of women dominating men. So many men have told me that they fantasize and masturbate with the thought of being dominated by a woman. Many men share intense submissive experience while watching films like *Basic Instinct, Cat Woman, Wonder Woman and Resident Evil,* or *older movies like, "My Tutor" or "Real Men".* Many men have told me that their first cravings for a dominant female came out of left field, when a dominant woman came upon the screen and caused them to experience an intense sexual arousal, unlike anything he had ever felt before. Why do movie, TV, magazine and other scenes of dominant women, have such a profound effect on some men? These scenes are powerful because the woman represents loving Female authority to these men. The women were often sweet and kind in public, but a real Bitch in private. She broke her male down through aggressive domination but then, was loving and nurturing toward him once he was broken. Like breaking a bucking bronco, until he submits to being ridden.

The reason Female Led Relationship stories, pictures and scenes in movies shake men at their core is because, they touch men at their core level of natural instincts. Their submissive nature becomes unleashed. It was there all the time, but they never knew it was there, until they discovered the world of the Female Led Relationship. Female Led Relationships did not invade their brains through pop culture, literature or the media. No, their submissive desires were there all the time, but those desires needed to be freed. A man's submissive nature has always been there, just concealed behind macho bravado; a false front which was really created by societal norms of the past. Once a man decides he wants to be submissive, it becomes perfectly natural. It could happen as a teenager later in life, when he no longer feels the pressure to conform to societal norms, and he can make his own decisions about what he wants. It generally also takes some maturity and life experience.

I believe that men generally, experience a powerful desire for a female leader, and have had this secret longing for a while, and something in previous relationships, or even childhood triggers it. Sometimes, this desire lays dormant until you trigger it. But men want to please their women; so most will be open to it. We only need to look at the search for "Female Domination" to see how many males are searching for the experience of being dominated by a woman. Today, there are literally thousands of websites, where women are offering to dominate men in person, or over the telephone. And more are coming on-line, all the time. The supply is growing because the demand is growing. There is a real societal evolution that is occurring, as the male desire to be dominated by the Female, is increasing at a rapid rate. Men will travel great distances and spend large amounts of money, just to find submissive fulfillment at the hands of a dominant woman. So, do not be timid and afraid to introduce your man to your dominant side in an exciting sexual event, or series of events, that build up over time.

CHAPTER SEVEN

---❦---

The Spirituality Of The Female Led Relationship

Women have been programmed, since they were little girls, that the natural order of God ordained institutions (Government, Religion and Family) is for men to be

dominant, and women to be submissive. Most religions teach that the male is the superior gender (made in the image of God) and thus, the man should rule the relationship. Are men spiritually superior to women? Is it by God's design that men should be the dominant gender in the society? Or have men perverted religion in order to keep women as second-class citizens? In Christianity, women are subservient. In the Muslim religion, women are practically non- existent, and not allowed to have the same rights and freedoms as males.

The three large patriarchal religions (Judaism, Christianity, and Islam) all trace their origins back to the Garden of Eden, with the belief that Adam and Eve were the original male and Female. Genesis is the recorded account of creation that most mainline religions and denominations use as the foundation of their faith. So, what does Genesis say about the original nature of man and woman?

In the story of Adam and Eve in the oldest Bible, it is said that Adam was created first, and Eve was created second. This was to try to suggest that this is why men are first, and had the power. But I see it another way. I see it as Adam was created and Eve was created second, as an improvement on the first creation, suggesting that women are the superior creation. Females tend to outlive men. There are many diseases which affect men greater than women, and women tend to be able to be strong, even in times of change and illness. When men went to war in World War I and World War II, the world did not come to an end. Women ran things. It is a fact that crime rates and atrocities in normal society decreased during these times as well. Perhaps, it's women's ability to go with the flow and intuition, which actually gives us the strength to be great leaders, especially in times of crisis.

Eve's subjection to Adam in the Bible was the result of the fall of mankind due to sin, and not God's original plan for Adam and Eve. Woman's subjection to man was called a curse in the Old Testament (Genesis 3:16-17). But the fact is, Eve gave Adam the fruit, but she did not hold a gun to his head and threaten him to eat it. He did it of his own free will, yet, women have been blamed for this original sin. I believe that what this shows is women's ability to influence men.

As I mentioned previously, the real lesson in this story is the power of the woman over men that made Adam disobey his God, to follow his wife's suggestion; hence, "happy wife, happy life" and showing that, even back then, women had real power. Though the Bible on one hand tries to condemn women, there are many instances where women are powerful. Another example is the Mother Mary, the most important woman in the bible for giving birth to baby Jesus. Even Delilah used her considerable influence to bring down the most powerful man Samson, who's been given strength by God. I personally believe that Eve was God's last and greatest creation, thus, women are the superior gender. I am not alone in this interpretation of the scriptures.

In addition to the three major religions, all have examples of powerful women; we are witnessing a return to many forms of Goddess Worship and religions. It has been estimated that in the United States alone, hundreds of thousands of people are now active in churches that believe in a Female deity. Most of these churches can trace their origin back to ancient civilizations, that actively worshipped a Goddess.

As far back, the Egyptians worshipped Isis, great Mother, Goddess of fertility, Giver of Life, and Queen Mother of Heaven. The Greeks worshipped Artemis, protectress of children, and the great Huntress; and the Romans worshipped Diana, Goddess of the moon and sister of Venus. Venus was originally Goddess of gardens and fields, later identified with Aphrodite, love and beauty. Worshipped as Venus Genetrix, mother of founder of Rome; Venus Felix, bringer of good fortune; Venus Victix, bringer of victory, and Venus Verticordia, protector of feminine chastity. Then, there is the Goddess Cybele. The name, Cybele or Cybebe, predominates in Greek and Roman literature from about the 5th century BC onward. Cybele was the Titan mother of the Olympian gods, who held domain over fertility and the earth. The Goddess Cybele held significance as a Goddess of the moon and of fertility, but was also worshipped in her earthly aspects as a fertility deity. The moon, throughout history, has been seen as a symbol of the feminine; its regular cycles correspond to the lifecycles of women. Three thousand years ago, the state religion of Phrygia (in what is now Turkey) was centered around the worship of the Mother Goddess there called Cybele. In many parts of the eastern Mediterranean, the Mother Goddess (under a variety of names), was served by a priesthood that often consisted of feminized males.

Other Goddesses worshipped throughout history were Aphrodite from Cyprus, Astarte from Phoenicia, Demeter from Mycenae, Ishtar from Assyria, Kali from India and Ostara, a Norse Goddess of fertility. Today, many in the western civilization look at such religions of old as being based on fables and mythology. Yet, many are joining New Age religions that center around the same beliefs of the Goddess religions of old, such as the worshipping of nature. Wicca is one of many earth-based religions. Traditional Wicca was founded by Gerald Gardner, a British civil slave, who wrote a series of books on the religion in the 1940's. It contains references to Celtic deities, symbols, and seasonal days of celebration. As a religion, Wicca is a reconstruction of the pre-Christian religions of Europe, especially Northern Europe (Celtic or Norse traditions), sometimes elsewhere, incorporating Greco-Roman and Egyptian traditions.

Many of our western Christian Holidays were in fact, founded as Goddess holidays. The Christmas holiday is an adaptation of the pagan winter solstice rites Yule; it was one of the traditional Celtic fire festivals, and marked the return of the light after the longest night of the year. Pagans (peasants, rustic people) in northwestern Europe, conducted a yearly celebration, which is remarkably similar to the Christmas we know today. The Christmas Tree is the left over from the pagan winter solstice rites. As Europe was evangelized by Christians, the pagan holiday was replaced with a Christian holiday, celebrating the birth of Christ. Most Biblical scholars believe that Christ was in fact, born in September, but since there was already a celebration in December, Christmas was substituted for Yule.

Easter is another Christian holiday that was originally based on Goddess worship. Easter was named after Eostre (a.k.a. Eastre). She was the Great Mother Goddess of the Saxon people in Northern Europe. Easter falls in the spring, right around the Vernal Equinox. Spring has been, and is, the season for much merrymaking and fun; much of the time with an emphasis on sexual fertility. Easter falls on the first Sunday, subsequent to the first full moon after the vernal equinox (March 21). Thus, it can occur as early as March 22nd, and as late as April 25th.

It has been argued, by those who are active in Goddess worship, that as women become more liberated, patriarchal religions will lose their appeal, and there will be a heavy return to Goddess religions of old. It has been my experience that the majority of couples who practice Female Led Relationship come from all religious affiliations, Christian, Jewish, Muslim, Buddhist, Goddess Worship, New Age, Agnostic and Atheist. A person's faith is a private matter, and most people are unwilling to change their Faith. I have known some dominant women who left the Christian Church and who have since, embraced Goddess religions, as they are more comfortable worshipping God as a female. But I also know many women that are active in the Female Led Relationship lifestyle, who are at ease with their Female Supremacy beliefs, and their Christian faith.

Dominant women, who are active in Christianity, will point out that their religion is not a patriarchal religion. Men have perverted it into a patriarchal religion, but Christianity is really about a personal relationship between a person and their Creator, through Christ. One need not change their religion when they have a revelation of the true natures of women and men. I chose to study my faith in more detail, to see if what I was being taught was indeed, so. I discovered that Christianity was very compatible with my Female Supremacy beliefs, and my Female Led Relationship lifestyle.

Why is all of this important? Because one of the major stumbling blocks for women when it comes to embracing the Female Led Relationship lifestyle is religion. Deep down, most women believe that they are equal or superior to males, but they still are uncomfortable with being in charge because of a feeling of guilt that religion has shackled them with since they were little girls. It is one thing to oppose a male dominant society based on Science or Ethics, but it is hard to oppose God or Nature. Religion uses fear and guilt to keep people enslaved to theologies that would otherwise, have no chance of surviving under the light of truth. Once the light of truth is shown and women begin to see that they are not going against their Maker or Nature by expressing or embracing being dominant, the shackles of religion can come off and the inner power of the Female can be exercised with a guilt-free mind, and a heart of confidence.

There is a spiritual dimension to Female Led Relationship. Females have a power over males, and that power is not physical. That power is expressed through the sexual, but it resides in the mind and originates in the spirit. This power is within, and women need to release it. I call this power the secret power of Eve. I believe that women were created to be in authority over men, not to lord it over them, but to complete them with loving Female authority. We are spiritual beings, so no matter how the mind has been programmed by society or religion, the spirit strives for truth. This may explain why man yearns for Female Led Relationship, even as he lives in a so-called patriarchal world.

CHAPTER EIGHT

--⊶⧟⊷--

Daily Practice of the Female Led Relationship

Now that you understand the history of Female Led Relationship and why your man craves this type of interaction, it's time to focus on the daily practice. To begin,

you need to get your man's attention. You need to step into the role of a Queen, and lead female. He needs to be thinking about you 24/7, and you need to create this desire in him by beginning with how you look, and how you conduct yourself in daily life. The best way to change old habits and get started, is to begin with your appearance. Men are visual and they are first, affected by what they see. Many of the most gorgeous women all agree that they continue to keep the attention of their husbands and boyfriends by always looking gorgeous, and visually appealing. I was always a t-shirt and jeans girl. It took a lot for me to come home, take care of chores, take a shower, and get dressed for my night with my partner. But, as I made this change, he noticed and the shift began. He naturally began to view me in a different light, and he changed how he treats me daily. This does not mean you need to go out and spend lots of money, but you do need to pay attention to how you look, hanging with your man. Sexy to me was gym clothes. I wore them everywhere I went - to the grocery store, out for coffee, to the movies, everywhere I went. Then I can recall the day most people witnessed me transformed in a suit, as a CEO, with full make-up, hair nails, every detail changed. It was not only the way my man looked at me, but it was the difference in the reception from everyone I encountered that made me realize the importance of what you present. The package you present the world is a snapshot of how you think of yourself. We can be smart, we can be successful and strong, but in the end, we affect the man in our life from the minute we wake up, to the minute we go to bed. What image do you want him to have in his mind? If you want your man to treat you as a Goddess, then you have to burn that image into his head, but being that image everyday of his life. Just this one change, he may not admit it immediately, but he will begin to secretly respect and adore you. Now, your first thought may be, "I don't have time to do all of this." But this is an excuse. We have time to put to watch TV and put on clothes, so we have time to put on the right clothes. It's one extra step which will help you to become more focused on your relationship, and he will become more focused on you. The saying, "The devil is in the details" could not be more true. It's the little things which will make the difference. Dress in your sexiest outfit out of the blue, and watch his reaction. Dress like the Goddess that you are, and watch the reaction from everyone around you. He will be taking notice, and that's the beginning of you exerting your power over him. This goes for those of us who are looking for a mate. When you go on a date, you have 10 minutes to impress this man. How will you get his attention over the other five dates he may have that week? You do it by exerting your Goddess power, right from the start. You wear something memorable, you take charge, you make him know that you will be in charge of the relationship, and that lingering impression will stay with him. I can recall when I first began to build social media for Female Led Relationships. My first post was about empowering women, and my first 50 followers were men. There is a demand for Female Led Relationships; men crave it, they want it. All you have to do now, is take control, and master the art of creating it. Next, you need to get your man into the habit of serving you first. When he comes home, give him a task. I instructed my man that no mater what, he finds me and he gives me a kiss. I also instructed that he sends me texts throughout the day, and he obeyed. Now, my man is focused on me throughout the day, and he can't wait to get home to be with his Goddess. These are practices which occur during courtship. Ever wonder why relationships are different during the first few months of a relationship? It's the anticipation, the focus on each other, the butterflies in the stomach. But these are all the things which can be re-created, but it takes work and a willingness for women to step into a new role. Your task is to keep your man serving you. Have him make you a drink, or put on some music. Spend some quality "play" time together. This is what couples are missing in general. The stresses and demands of daily life take precedence. Just as we build in time for fitness and work, we must build in time for the relationship. I send my man off with a compliment, everyday. I began this practice years ago. He has no one else to compliment him, so if you don't do it, no one can. The only person in your man's life who can lift him up, is you. This is the same for the man you want to date, or you are attracted to. Lift him up, compliment him, make him the focus over all other dates, and he will be yours. When we are young and first exploring dating and relationships, women make the mistake of always giving. We are givers by nature, so we feel that if we give and give and give, we will get our man. This is not always true because it opens the door to the man treating you like a doormat. You can give- give instructions, give love, give attention, as opposed to giving your soul or your body or your life goals. There is a difference. A woman can still conduct her own life, and be very available for her man, and only allows him to have her when she chooses. This is the power position. As opposed to the feeling that you have to have sex or tend to his needs before your own. When you are building a Female Led Relationship, you must identify the times when you are allowing your needs to be cast aside, and insist that your man attend to you first.

I have done this everyday in my relationship, and it has transformed it into a complete fulfillment for both of us. He enjoys the opportunity to tend to my needs first, and it helps him to feel manliness by taking charge in this. Let's face it; we are human beings. We all want love and appreciation. No one can offer this to your man better than you.

Then, once you have him to that magical place of submission, change your behavior. Become soft, hold him, kiss him, and compliment him. Ask him how was his day. Listen attentively, and refrain from any criticism. The same for you; when you discuss your day, you are just keeping the conversation open. Less venting, more flow. If you start to feel like making-love, make the natural transition, but be sure to control the flow. Make him serve you and do the things you want, first. He will appreciate you. Many women fail to adequately inform their man of what they really want, but this is your opportunity. Allow yours and his deepest desires to come out, but you control the moment. He satisfies you first, then slowly, you allow him to have his pleasure. Sometimes, I would instruct my man to hold back his orgasm to build his willpower but sometimes, I order him to just be intense and fast in our love-making. But, I control every moment of our time together. The more encouraging you are, the more he will open up. You will come to understand him more than you ever thought was possible. Comfort him. Speak to him like his Queen -

"Baby, I know that you have searched your entire life to find your rightful place, which is to be in complete submission to me. Well, your search is over. I am here, and I am here to stay. I want you to surrender yourself to me. Your mind, your body, your ego, your everything." Men love this. They love hearing their women speak about taking control, then watching the actions as well. Then he knows you are serious, and can give you his undivided attention.

Experiment as much as you can, always maintaining your Queen mother role and leader. Never let him disrespect you, but if he does, correct him, so he knows it's not permitted. I have had many challenges with this, particularly in public, when my man slips and issues me orders. Instead of being upset, I simply remind him that he takes my lead at all times. He may not say anything, but it helps to build the practice. At all points, make him know that he has to love and obey you. This must be daily and slowly; so he becomes accustomed. It must extend into a lifestyle. In the early stages of relationships during the dating period, you want to establish the foundation early. Instruct that he calls, and be available to speak at a certain time. Instruct him to wait for you to decide where you will go for dinner. Let him know early on, that you require him to open doors, to allow you to enter first, pull out your chair, and help you with your coat. Many women are fearful of starting at this point but, it's best that you establish what you want, right from the start. Building good habits together and re- inforcing the rules will go a long way to making sure he understands what is expected of him. It will help you to also determine if it's possible for your man to go long-term. Balancing work with your Female Led Relationship practice will become essential. You need to greet your man, as enthusiastically as you would, on your day off. Your behavior as queen has to occur whether you are stressed out, trying to complete work deadlines, taking care of kids, elderly parents, or attending to your own personal responsibilities. This could be a challenge because often, when couples have been together for a long time, the relationship becomes secondary. Planning and building the daily habits help you and your man to maintain the relationship, despite what is happening. Greeting you with a kiss or bringing home some flowers randomly, will become the norm. It keeps the focus squarely on the relationship, even if daily tasks and demands become overwhelming. Domination in the bedroom is a must. You must take the lead to initiate sex. This will be very exciting to your man who may have never had it happen. This is how you establish leadership.

What you will eventually notice is that if you dominate a man in the bedroom, this can lead to a man's submission outside of the bedroom. He will be constantly thinking about you, every time you take the lead in daily life. This can add a refreshing, exciting spin on things. You will find that the more you allow your dominant Queen role to takeover, the more empowered you will feel, and the happier you will be, because it adds a dimension to all aspects of your life that you don't normally experience. You could experience a more intense sex life too because your bond increases with your man. It's only a plus when you both can't wait to come home to be together. In my experience, you want to now take it to the next level by taking the initiative during the day; maintain your influence over your man. Send him love messages and texts, or random racy pictures, or make a spontaneous romantic date. I insisted on the daily practice of sending my man texts, and he reciprocated by doing the same. Not a day goes by where we don't send sexy texts, or just an "I love you" emoji. It helps to keep the connection throughout the day. Just because daily life happens doesn't mean your relationship has to fade. The Female Led Relationship can improve all aspects of life. More confidence in career, other friendships and relationships, and general outlook. I noticed more positivity from women in Female Led Relationships, and a general sense of happiness. They lead to stronger marriages because most men would agree with the saying, "Happy wife, Happy life." I can personally report a major change in my relationships; each day presents an exciting new challenge to please each other, rather than more boredom. Female led relationships are anything but boring, because each day is a new chance to take things to a new level. The learning that happens in these relationships, I feel, surpasses what happens in traditional ones, provided it's a positive flow. The danger is to try to rush or force your man into this relationship. It must make a natural flow. What is important though, is as a leader, you must continue to evolve, learn, and encounter challenges head-on. You cannot be afraid to take the reign into your own hands, no matter what. In challenging times, or arguments, continue to maintain your queen's presence. Calm him down by always maintaining an open channel of communication. Refrain from criticism of any sort, and work with both yours and his weaknesses. The Female Led Relationship does not need to be perfect. It's a learning experience everyday.

So, start out slowly. Simply start with getting your man to begin treating you like a Queen. Teach him at first, to be a gentleman. Allow him open the door for you, pull out your chair at dinner, take your coat off when you return home, and act like a real gentleman around you. Enforce this as your new rules! Tell him that you want him to surprise you with flowers and gifts of appreciation on a regular basis and then, reward him with great sex. Soon, he will be conditioned to know that his proper treatment of you results in sexual rewards, and he will keep desiring to increase his rewards by being more obedient and serving you better, all the time. Tell him that you are most appreciative of this new attention, and respond with warm reactions and affection to the man's warm actions. You will see how fast this will re-kindle the romance in your relationship. Do not permit bad habits of ignoring you, being on the phone at important intimate times, watching endless TV with no conversation. Do not go an entire day without some intimate touching. A simple kiss, holding hands, stroking his hair - these are all necessary daily actions which must happen. Encourage it;

that way, you are reinforcing the training each day. Sometimes, I will add a different request everyday, to keep my man in the habit of serving me. He enjoys the attention, and I keep him in the mode of submitting to my lead. You must set the rules; make him focus on ways to serve you and bring you pleasure. If you work on your feet most of the day, teach your man to get in the mode of serving his Queen Mother. Make him kneel at your feet, remove your shoes, and give you a tender-loving foot massage.

Then reward him with intimacy, with the pleasure being controlled and directed by you. Instruct your man to help with the chores around the house. Women usually have to beg and nag a man to mow the lawn, wash the cars, and to put out the trash on garbage night. If your man doesn't enjoy doing household chores, you must change his mind set by making him realize that by doing these chores, he is serving his Queen, and he will be rewarded. Soon, your man will really be enjoying his status of being your gentleman. Don't always try to be supermom or superwoman. Allow your man to help you. This way, you create a collaboration. When he is well-trained, he will even jump in and help you with some of the so-called woman's chores, like washing dishes, vacuuming and dusting.

Your man's continued servitude of you will seduce your dominant nature. Women have dominant urges, but they suppress it because of how we were raised. Many women still believe that to be happy, a woman needs to marry a strong man and then, allow the man to wear the pants in the family. Even for the most Macho men, it won't take long, after your relationship starts, for them to realize that a woman can take the lead. They may come to enjoy giving you the control. What is evident is that the Female Led Relationship is the next evolution, and more and more couples are embracing it. As women become more powerful in the society, the more the role of leadership is perfect for you. What is important is positive encouragement, openness and patience. It is a transition for both men and women; so, allowing the relationship to unfold at its own pace will be important. Taking a leadership role may still seem daunting because of childhood conditioning from religion or parental rules. However, women are taking leadership roles in career, heads of state and media; so, it's only natural they can lead in the bedroom. There is very little to suggest that women are inferiors, and lots of evidence to prove that they are in fact, superior. It is my hope that you will find great fulfillment in your Female Led Relationship after practicing all the advice in this book. It is my wish that all women and men enjoy this movement, and use it to create more fulfilling and long-lasting relationships.

About the Author

Marisa Rudder was born in the Caribbean. She moved to Toronto, Canada, where she attended McMaster University, studied Chemical Engineering, before going on to study Information Technology and Commerce at Ryerson University. Both fields were intensely make- dominated at the time where women had to fight to be heard and accepted. It is at this time that Marisa developed her ideas of Female equality, and even superiority, as she witnessed hers and the struggle of many of her female associates and friends.

Marisa admits to also struggling with her weight and self-esteem, as she ballooned to 210lbs at her heaviest. It is then that she made the firm decision to put her needs first, and take control of her life, beginning with diet and lifestyle. She focused on fitness, joined a local gym, and began the transformation of her body, and went from 201lbs to 135lbs in 6 months. She became so passionate about this new lifestyle, which boost her self-esteem, and she studied and became one of the top certified Personal Trainers in North America, training everyone, from celebrities to CEO's. It is during this time, while she interacted with many powerful women and men, she began to solidify her ideas about Female Led Relationships. She continued her evolution onto the stage where her love of theater led her to perform in Toronto's off-Broadway theatre world. She has performed in starring roles on stage, in front of sell-out crowds in theatrical productions of the Lion King, Sister Act, Willy Wonka and Peter Pan. She credits this experience with watching women take charge when they came together to run non-profit campaigns to feed thousands of orphans in Africa.

Today, Marisa shows no signs of slowing down. She made the decision to go back into the world of IT and the Internet, where she now heads up and is CEO of Quantum Ad Ventures Inc. a global TV and Internet production and marketing company based in Toronto, with clients in Europe, America, the Middle East and Asia. All of this experience has led to her decision to become an author, writing books and spreading her message about the benefits of Female Led Relationships, and the new power females.

She expects that this is just the beginning of a revolution for women.